THE
ALPHA
HUNTER

Profiting from
Option LEAPS

JASON SCHWARZ

New York Chicago San Francisco Lisbon London
Madrid Mexico City Milan New Delhi San Juan
Seoul Singapore Sydney Toronto

The *McGraw-Hill* Companies

To my wonderful wife, Kelli Ann:
your love and encouragement make all things possible.

1 2 3 4 5 6 7 8 9 0   DOC/DOC   0 1 0 9

ISBN: 978-0-07-163408-3
MHID: 0-07-163408-8

This publication is designed to provide accurate and authoritative information in regard to the subject matter covered. It is sold with the understanding that the publisher is not engaged in rendering legal, accounting, futures/securities trading, or other professional service. If legal advice or other expert assistance is required, the services of a competent professional person should be sought.

—*From a declaration of principles jointly adopted by a committee of the American Bar Association and a committee of publishers.*

McGraw-Hill books are available at special quantity discounts to use as premiums and sales promotions, or for use in corporate training programs. To contact a representative please visit the Contact Us pages at www.mhprofessional.com.

CONTENTS

introduction

THE ELEMENTS OF
AN ALPHA HUNTER

The recession of 2007 to 2009 has ushered in a host of new market variables. The president of the United States is intent on upending the status quo in a way we haven't seen since the Reagan Revolution. We will exit the recession with a reformed financial sector, a reforming automotive sector, and likely with a health care sector on the verge of radical transformation. Already digital technology has infiltrated and interconnected our society in ways beyond what all but the brightest dot-com investors of 1999 envisioned. Cyberroads of high-speed 3G and 4G wireless Internet have sparked a quantum jump in the breadth of communication: "tomorrow the world" is a boast of the past. As the world slowly recovers from the recent economic disasters, investors must absorb the implications of these massive changes, which have done nothing less than kick us all into a new world with new rules.

I feel fortunate to be working as an options strategist in such a volatile and exciting time. Options strategists are something like Special Forces members—the Green Berets or the Navy SEALs—to investors. We are trained to identify market opportunities and to take direct action. We understand how to profit from special situations in ways that the average investor doesn't have the time or means to master.

As with most professions, sophisticated options trading doesn't happen simply as a result of good academic training; it needs to be rooted in street smarts. If you want to know where the market is headed, you'd better talk to an options strategist.

I was trained by a master of option LEAPS investing whose innovative approach helped me develop a clear eye for the challenges presented by the new Wall Street. Since 2000, this market has abandoned its established, rigid patterns, and it is in the process of setting new precedents of volatility. The insights contained within these pages will help you navigate the new patterns, or the lack of them, whether you're out to improve as a LEAPS investor or simply to better understand the general motions of the stock market.

I've been studying the investment world for as long as I can remember. One of my earliest, sharpest instructors was Wilma Rosenberg, my second-grade teacher, who tasked our class with collecting and recycling thousands of empty aluminum cans and using the proceeds to buy one share of Disney stock. (She had us convinced that with one share of Disney we would be owners of our favorite place in the world, Disneyland!) She instructed us to track that ticker symbol in the newspaper every morning until we came up with the $60 we needed to buy our share (not a bad investment by the way: adjusted for splits, the stock has risen 557 percent since then). Don't think it's easy to make $60 from recycling cans at

$0.02 per can refund. My buddies and I had to swill gallons of Dad's Root Beer in order to reach our quota; and I became and remain an expert at the one-stomp soda can squish.

I had to fight off a sugar addiction after that, but more importantly Mrs. Rosenberg got me hooked on stocks. It's still exciting to think that I can be a shareholder in any publicly held company I want. The liquidity of ownership is what makes stock investing the greatest profession in the world. The freedom to enter and exit positions is more profound that most realize.

Since I was a kid, I've compiled a list of people who, if you combined their key characteristics, would create the greatest investor of all time. While this "greatest investor" amalgam is perpetually a work in progress, I'm going to share it now, before we discuss the specifics of my investment strategy, because it incorporates the basic tools you'll need to outperform the new Wall Street. We're in an era of unprecedented volatility, but we're lucky that there are still plenty of excellent lessons to be culled from the past.

So without further ado, I now present you with my nine exemplary elements of general investment theory.

Element 1: Interpret Reality and Make Something Happen—John F. Kennedy

Nobody took advantage of the present like our thirty-fifth president, John F. Kennedy. This was a man ahead of his time. Consider that President Kennedy was traveling by private jet and helicopter in the technologically inferior 1960s while you and I are still stuck in freeway traffic in 2010. It's easy to be distracted by his vices and the cult of personality that surrounds him in death as it did in life, but there always was much more substance to the man than the cool persona that he used to captivate the world.

I believe Kennedy's legacy has grown, to a great extent, out of three of his abilities. First, he was able to recognize when current norms of human behavior had negative impacts. This is never a simple thing if you're a leader because you have to stand against the crowd. But it was precisely this ability that allowed him to enable the Civil Rights movement and have a real impact on ending racial injustices in our country. Traditionalists were never his fans, but he had the intellectual capacity to identify the wrongs of the past and the courage to act on his belief in the present.

Second, he never relied on stereotypes to define how cultures differ from one another. Before being elected to public office, JFK made a point of traveling abroad to learn about what made each nation tick. Effective foreign policy presumes that a traveler's own culture is just as "foreign" to outsiders as the foreign culture is to the traveler. American diplomats are guaranteed to offend when they act under false assumptions, and Kennedy made certain he never did.

Third, by refusing to accept the limitations of the past, JFK lived in real time and took advantage of the opportunities in front of him. He helped launch a space program that put a man on the moon not even six years after his death. He took care of the poor. He halted the Cuban missile crisis. Undeniably his achievements were aided by opportunities created by his family money, athleticism, and good communication skills, but his true gift was his ability to achieve in the present and ignore false information.

There's plenty in the JFK biography that is of immediate value to the alpha investor. We must have a real understanding of the events going on around us. We need our own effective foreign policy on the new Wall Street; globalization is an economic variable that has never been more powerful than it is today.

New variables insinuate themselves into society slowly—and with such little disturbance that we don't feel the need to immediately adapt in the short run, even when long-run adaptations are necessary to continued success. This is exactly what has happened on Wall Street. Small changes have crept incrementally into the daily workings of the market; and the only investors succeeding are those who work to understand new dynamics in the same way that JFK did.

Element 2: Become a Seer—Steve Jobs

Nobody sees the future like Apple CEO Steve Jobs. He has earned the reputation as a "seer" over 30 years, starting with his revolutionary work with computers in the 1970s. In the 1980s, he unveiled Apple 2 and the Mac; in the 1990s, animated movies with Pixar; in the 2000s, digital music with the iPod; and before the 2010s hit, we've got the iPhone reinventing the smart phone market and a touch Mac Tablet device on the horizon. Where would we be without this guy? How does he do it? If you could project future trends the way Steve Jobs does, investing would be a cakewalk. Give us some answers, Steve!

Well, he did. In an interview with *Rolling Stone*, Jobs spilled his secret: "You can't really predict exactly what will happen, but you can feel the direction that we're going. And that's about as close as you can get [to predicting the future]. Then you just stand back and get out of the way, and these things take on a life of their own." Jobs said he looks for "vectors going in time": what new technologies are coming to market, which ones are ending their run. "You try and spot those things and how they're going to be changing over time and which horses you want to ride at any point in time. You can't be too far ahead, but you have to be far enough ahead, because it takes time to implement. So you have to intercept a moving train."

In a separate interview with *Wired* magazine, Jobs provided some more insight into becoming a seer: "When you ask creative people how they did something, they feel a little guilty because they didn't really do it, they just saw something. It seemed obvious to them after a while. That's because they were able to connect experiences they've had and synthesize new things. And the reason they were able to do that was that they've had more experiences or they have thought more about their experiences than other people. . . . Unfortunately that's too rare a commodity."[1]

Becoming an investment seer depends on one's ability to identify the economic direction and the velocity of a variable. Once you are established on the correct path, you will be able to spend your time making creative connections that result in innovation and achievement. If you're stuck on an incorrect path, your sight will become blurred beyond belief.

To become an investment seer, one mustn't be too far ahead, but you have to be far *enough* ahead to take part in the stock price action. (Those who want to become seers will especially enjoy Chapter 3).

Element 3: Know the Uncertain Mysteries of the Market — J.J. Abrams

Positive uncertainty will cause a stock to soar; negative uncertainty will cause a stock to plummet. J.J. Abrams is arguably the most relevant American film and television producer, screenwriter, and director in the entertainment industry today. He created the hit television series *Lost*, he directed the renaissance of *Star Trek*, and he has worked on multiple other projects that have generated millions upon million of dollars in revenue. Abrams is guided by a philosophy he calls the "mystery box." As a young boy, he purchased a mystery box from a magic store, with $50 worth of tricks hidden inside. Unlike most kids on planet Earth, he never opened the box because its infinite possibility, its untapped potential, would vanish as soon as his eyes saw its contents. That magic box still sits unopened on a shelf in his office. As soon as the mystery is solved, there is no more intrigue.[2]

Mystery is a powerful catalyst for movie production, but it has an intriguing influence on investing as well. In a world that strives for transparency, the element of surprise can create some wild movements in a stock. We'll all remember what the negative uncertainty created by the financial crisis did to the overall market in 2008, but uncertainty does work both ways. I love finding a stock with some sort of unresolved question swirling around it. More often than not, the expectation sparked by the mystery will supersede an actual event. You can find mystery stocks with upside potential during an improving economy, and you can find mystery stocks with downside potential in a worsening economy. The appeal of positive uncertainty will take a stock up faster than any other investment variable.

While we're talking about J.J. Abrams, I want to add one other golden nugget: he knows that viewers enjoy shows that are character driven. In a sequel it's easy for producers to believe that the continuation of the previous story line is more important than the character development, , but it's not. The same principle applies to company stocks and their products. Companies are built upon individual products and services, and they experience change in management—sequels—from time to time. As soon as management forgets that its growth is derived from great products, that company is no longer worth investing in. Look at the American automotive industry to see what I mean. General Motors' product mix got so watered down that eventually it lost its identity and its products' appeal. You can never forget that excellent products are key to a stock's viability.

Element 4: Ask the Right Questions—David Frost

The interview David Frost conducted with Richard Nixon after his resignation was a dramatic event for both participants and the nation as well. Frost was hoping to rejuvenate his declining career, while Nixon was desperate to resurrect his image in the aftermath of Watergate. Nixon accepted Frost's offer of $600,000 in return for a 28-hour interview, during which Frost could ask him anything he wanted.

Frost was out to extract information that Nixon had so far withheld from the public. Nixon, always aware that Frost was working against the clock, tried to use up airtime by telling old stories, usually off topic. It was not unlike a heavyweight match, and it captivated 45 million viewers, a record for a broadcast interview.

Ultimately, Nixon admitted his belief that "when the President does it, that means it's not illegal." Frost had managed to ask the right questions and finally extracted the detail the entire nation wanted to know.[3]

Knowing how to ask the right question at the right time can make you a lot of money as an investor. It might even be more important than the ability to sort through and analyze fundamental data. It's interesting how the right question can totally deflate an investment thesis or propel it to new heights.

To my thinking, the greatest question asked in the last 10 years was this: "Has the banking industry ever had to live with mark-to-market regulatory requirements before?" Well, yes, it has. It existed during the Great Depression, until President Roosevelt repealed it in 1938! For approximately 70 years, banks had operated without mark-to-market accounting, and the economy didn't have the threat of another depression. Milton Friedman wrote that mark-to-market accounting was responsible for the avoidable failure of many banks in the 1930s. Is there a correlation between the reinstitution of mark-to-market on November 15, 2007, and the recession's beginning in the very same month? Do you think it's simply coincidental that signs of recovery proliferated when that accounting regulation was altered on March 3, 2009? You be the judge.[4]

Element 5: Be Efficient with Your Research—John Wooden

Legendary UCLA basketball coach John Wooden won 10 NCAA National Championships in 12 years and was greatly admired for his religious and personal values. There is ample testimony that there was no division between those values and his coaching skills, including that of former player Bill Walton and former assistant coach Denny Crum:

> John Wooden is the greatest basketball coach of all time, but what I learned from him had much more to do with living life than with playing ball. He taught us how to focus on one primary objective: Be the best you can be in whatever endeavor you undertake. Don't worry about the score. Don't worry about image. Don't worry about the opponent. It sounds easy, but it's actually very difficult. Coach Wooden showed us how to accomplish it. You saw how true he was to doing things right, by thinking right. Coach was more interested in the process than the result.[5]
>
> —Bill Walton

> As an assistant coach under Coach Wooden, I learned more about organizing your time, planning, evaluating, and teaching than in all my years of college put together. He was a master at organizing what needed to be done down to the last detail and then teaching it the same way. I believe his longevity at the top of the college basketball ladder was no accident.[6]
>
> —Denny Crum

I try to emulate Wooden's attention to relevant details whenever I'm engaged in investment research. I've always been motivated by his efficiency and equal devotion to the process *and* the final result.

All too often the investment profession defines *work* as a noun, not a verb. It's often assumed that a good work ethic means nothing less than regular 14-hour days. I think nothing could be further from the truth. Whenever I hear about some hedge fund manager who works so much that he sleeps at the office, I think about basketball coaches who punish their teams with 5-hour practices. At some point, the unrelenting approach to work actually becomes unproductive.

Element 6: Bounce Back—George Washington

The first president of the United States was no stranger to sorrow, cold, hunger, persecution, violence, or terrorism. Washington's great accomplishment was to face misfortune and conquer it; he achieved victory by discipline, commitment, and prayer. "It will not be believed that such a force as Great Britain has employed for eight years in Country could be baffled . . . by numbers infinitely less, composed of men oftentimes half starved; always in rags, without pay, and experiencing at times every species of distress which human nature is capable of undergoing."[7]

David McCullough, in his book *1776*, quotes a young officer who served under General Washington at the Battle of Princeton and who gave an eye-witness account of the commander in chief under attack: "I shall never forget what I felt . . . when I saw him brave all the dangers of the field and his important life hanging as it were by a single hair with a thousand deaths flying around him."[8]

If Washington had given up, Americans might still be British subjects. If you or I give up, we lose our chance to become the nation's greatest investor. If he could hold his resolve in matters of life and death, certainly we can keep steady even when the market doesn't. Perhaps nothing is more important in life than getting back up after you've been knocked down. Investing can be cruel; a rereading of Washington's hardships, and his response to them, will be of great help in the tight spots.

Element 7: Let the Superstars Do Their Thing—Tommy Lasorda and Kirk Gibson

As a sports enthusiast, I have been fortunate to attend some great games in my lifetime, but no game was greater than game one of the 1988 World Series.

My Dad and I headed down to Chavez Ravine to cheer on our underdog Dodgers against the mighty Oakland A's. In all honesty, most Dodger fans just were happy to be *in* the World Series; the A's, a real powerhouse, were heavily favored. Sure enough, they got a monster, sixth-inning grand slam from MVP Jose Canseco. In the ninth they had a 4-to-3 lead and Dennis Eckersley, perhaps the most dominant closer in history, on the mound. I was actually *afraid* of Eckersley, with his long hair and unorthodox, slingshot delivery; in 1988, one of his best seasons, I'd bet most Major League hitters feared him too.

Fans were already starting to file out of the ballpark to avoid the traffic. Dad and I kept walking lower and lower to get better seats for the finale. Eckersley got two quick outs, but then, uncharacteristically, he walked a guy. He gave us a glimmer of hope. With the winning run at the plate, the Dodger's manager, Tom Lasorda, made one of the best decisions in the history of the game and sent Kirk Gibson up to pinch-hit.

Although he had carried the team all year, by now Gibson was a physical wreck, hobbling because of recent injuries to both legs.

That at-bat was to be his only appearance in the series, but the transcript of broadcaster Vin Scully's play-by-play explains why people will always remember it:

> And [Eckersley] walked [pinch-hitter Mike Davis] . . . and look who's comin' up!
>
> [36 seconds of crowd cheering]
>
> . . . With two out, you talk about a roll of the dice . . . this is it. If he hits the ball on the ground, I would imagine he would be running 50 percent to first base. So, the Dodgers trying to catch lightning right now!
>
> . . . Gibson, shaking his left leg, making it quiver, like a horse trying to get rid of a troublesome fly. 2-and-2! Tony LaRussa is one out away from win number one.
>
> . . . High fly ball into right field, she i-i-i-is . . . gone!!
>
> [67 seconds of cheering]
>
> In a year that has been so improbable . . . the impossible has happened!
>
> And, now, the only question was, could he make it around the base paths unassisted?!
>
> . . . They are going wild at Dodger Stadium—no one wants to leave![9]

Tommy Lasorda knew enough to trust his superstar even when he was weakened by injuries. The same lesson can be applied to investing: you don't give up on your star stocks. A lack of productive patience can damage a portfolio. A good investor knows when to let his or her stocks ride. Even when the present price movement in unpleasant to watch, you let your known superstars do their thing. Like Gibson, they're worthless if you don't put them in the game. The key is to know when patience will pay off and when it won't; my rules of investing, outlined in Chapter 5, will show you how.

Element 8: Follow the Symbols—Robert Langdon

We're surrounded by symbols and archetypes. They pass through our hands every day, and often we miss them. You can infer a great deal about the principles that help structure our nation just by stopping to look at the symbols that cover our currency, presidential seal, and flag: the portraits, the bald eagle, the stars and stripes. Nature itself is conveyed through symbols such as the sunrise and sunset. Each symbol is a portal to a message of much greater depth than its literal, superficial meaning. If you don't understand the symbol, you risk missing the main chance.

Dan Brown has sold more than 150 million copies of *The Da Vinci Code*, *Angels and Demons*, and *The Lost Symbol*, all of which feature a Harvard symbologist, Robert Langdon, as a hero who uncovers the universal meaning of ancient symbols. Langdon's adventures are great fun, but I personally am not a devotee of fiction. I prefer the real stuff.

Stock investing is informed by the art of interpreting real-life symbols and determining what those symbols reveal about the health of the global economy. For all of you wannabe symbologists out there who are itching to crack a code, investing is for you. If you can properly interpret collective life experience and identify the associated symbols, you will be able to outperform the market.[10]

Every stock has a ticker symbol, and every symbol stands for something beyond its associated company. These symbols serve as a guide to understanding where the various sectors of the economy are headed. If society has experienced technological progression, it will be "symbolized" by an uptick in tech stocks. If society has overindulged on credit, that behavior will manifest itself in the symbolic weakness of bank stocks. The stock market serves as a modern-day weather station for the cycles of human progress or regression.

Becoming a successful alpha hunter is dependent on becoming well versed in sociological symbology. A numeric understanding of stocks should serve only to reinforce a sociological thesis. To become a successful investor, you need to gather information you may not have believed was important. Simply memorizing statistics or reading all of the media commentary in the world won't be sufficient to outperform on Wall Street. The symbols of stocks give conceptual form to the behavior of consumers, governments, and global societies.

Stocks are used to communicate complex ideas about the future in their price action of the present. The mistake that so many investors make is that they expect a stock to be priced based on past events or current data. It would be an easy profession to master if that were the case. In reality, the stock market is a crystal ball, a forward-looking entity that contains symbols of future performance. Sometimes past or current data can influence some characteristic of the market, but other times it's already priced in. This helps explain the origin of the saying "Buy on the rumor, sell on the news."

The easy way to write an investment book is to keep the content purely academic and in line with the norms of finance. I could fill the pages with rigid investment rules and make guarantees of mechanical, reliable success. I could come up with all sorts of fancy charts and graphs that make me appear intelligent but hardly scratch the surface of what it takes to achieve real-world success. Instead, I'm going to try to shift your perspective until it includes not only the here and now but the past and the future as well. Investors are often frustrated when the market doesn't perform as anticipated, but many times the fault can be traced to their limited perception of how things *really* are.

Can anybody know *everything* about the future? Of course not, but this book will show you how the market prices in and anticipates the future before it arrives. It's information that can be delivered only through symbols.

Element 9: Achieve Alpha—Keane

What is alpha? In the investing world, *alpha* refers to a stock's performance relative to the market. Fund managers often employ it as a descriptive term when they beat their benchmark index. But to drive the meaning home, allow me to illustrate with some rock 'n' roll.

Every music fan has found a band that becomes more than a sum of parts when it performs; this is a group so talented that it coalesces into a unit that includes not only each member but also the audience it's playing for. I discovered an ensemble with that kind of talent just recently, when I attended a Keane concert.

For those unfamiliar with the band, Keane has drawn comparisons to legends like Coldplay and U2. The band is a British foursome, and while I'm sure people who actually *saw* the Beatles (and plenty who never did) would call me blasphemous, I suspect the energy at the concert I attended was similar to what the Fab Four whipped up back in the 1960s. With pristine vocals and startling musical chops, these guys kept up the energy from start to finish, with everyone in the audience leaping about, dancing, and singing along.

What Keane accomplished at that concert fits my definition of alpha. The moving parts from each individual musician came together into one dazzling whole. It's funny that I wasn't much of a Keane fan before last week, and now I'm writing them into my first investment book, but that's what alpha does. It's instantly recognizable. Alpha is the ability to harness the tools at your disposal into a result that surpasses expectations.

I think the goal of all great people—whether they are musicians, athletes, school teachers, mechanics, you name it— is to optimize the tools at their disposal. The term *alpha* is used in biology to identify the dominant animal in a community; in aviation it's a term for the proper angle of attack; in mathematics it's a statistic of reliability. To buy the right stock at the right time gives me the same sensation that Lebron James gets from hitting a game-winning shot, or a teacher gets from connecting with a student. Achieving alpha in any arena is exhilarating.

Those are my nine elements of investment success. A daily review of each one will help to get your mind in the right zone as you assess your portfolio and make investment decisions. You can condense them by following this checklist:

1. Does my portfolio fit with the JKF-like interpretation of reality? What inconsistencies in the status quo am I trying to

take advantage of? Am I situated for the latest trends of globalization? Does my portfolio have a productive game plan?

2. Would Steve Jobs agree that this particular holding is a horse I want to be riding at this point in time? Am I early, or am I late? Have I correctly identified the direction we are headed?

3. What are today's J.J. Abrams uncertainties? Is uncertainty working for me, or is it working against me?

4. What is the market-moving question of the day? Does the answer unveil something new about this market that changes my past assumption?

5. What research can I conduct today that will efficiently utilize my time? I want today to be as productive as it would be for a guard practicing with John Wooden.

6. Do I have the courage to remain true to my convictions? If I'm waffling, it's time to bounce back. What adjustments do I need to make?

7. Is this a time for my superstar stocks to be in the game? Are my best stocks in a position to achieve their potential, or do they need to sit on the bench a little longer?

8. Have I selected the correct symbols that properly represent this economy? If my symbols aren't representative of underlying societal trends, than which ones are?

9. Is my portfolio an alpha portfolio? Am I using the investment tools at my disposal to best achieve my portfolio objectives?

one

THE NEW WALL STREET

In August 2008, the global spotlight was shining on the New Wall Street as never before, not least because the price of a barrel of oil was galloping up to its peak of $147. At the time, I wrote an article for the Seeking Alpha Web site in which I predicted that not only would this commodity run not last but also that oil was in for a gigantic drop in price: it would return not to $100 a barrel, but to its historic norm of $30 to $50 a barrel, and it would get there within a year.

That was a forecast that got people talking. My article was the most popular on Seeking Alpha for at least three weeks, and soon it was circulating through China, Russia, and the Middle East. The major television networks took notice, and they invited me on for interviews in which I discussed my thesis. In an age when it's increasingly hard to make one's voice heard above the collective, daily roar of the mass media, I'd had a breakthrough.

But as I did my tour of the television studios, it was obvious that my newfound popularity wasn't based on respect for my prediction; if anything, it was considered so outrageous as to provide good entertainment. I could see that my interviewers didn't agree with me and perhaps didn't even take me seriously.

And why should they? The experts in the field—billionaire oilman T. Boone Pickens, the legendary Goldman Sachs investment firm, to name a couple—were predicting that oil was going to keep going up, perhaps to $200 a barrel. History had become an unreliable guideline; high oil was the new norm. Who was I to suggest otherwise?[1]

Well, I was an analyst coming from another perspective, an outsider's perspective. Most analysts, such as Pickens and Goldman Sachs, have conflicts of interest. Much of Pickens' vast fortune was invested in oil and alternative energy.

Goldman Sachs was generating huge returns in its commodity trading department. These were players positioned to clean up should the price of oil continue its upward march. How did that affect their judgment?

Months later, in January 2009, hedge fund manager Michael Masters commented on the unusual oil speculation activity in a *60 Minutes Special Report.* "So you had the largest price increase in history during a time when actual demand was going down and actual supply was going up during the same period," he said. He concluded that the only sensible explanation for the jump in price "was investor demand."

Masters believed that investor demand for commodities, and oil futures in particular, was created on Wall Street by hedge funds and the big investment banks, such as Morgan Stanley, Goldman Sachs, Barclays, and J.P. Morgan, which made billions investing their clients' money. "The investment banks facilitated it," Masters said. "You know, they found folks to write papers espousing the benefits of investing in commodities. And then they promoted commodities as a, quote-unquote, 'asset class.' Like, you could invest in commodities just like you could in stocks or bonds or anything else, like they were suitable for long-term investment."[2]

In the summer of 2008, contagious momentum had infected the commodities market and created an overreaction that reached bubble proportions and spread across the spectrum of analysts and commentators. Once you're inside a bubble, it is easy to lose sight of the big picture. That's why no one in the financial media agreed with me. And it wasn't just them; even my own family and friends thought that my oil call was crazy.

But you know how the story ends. Within a few short, wild months, crude was at $30 a barrel.

That was my first chance to play out a David and Goliath scenario with traditional Wall Street. Then, in March 2009, I spelled out a thesis on TheStreet.com in which I argued that financial stocks were ready to rally off of the bottom. The primary article, titled "Bank of America Is Going Back to $20," was published the day Bank of America hit its low of $2.53.[3]

Again, it was the right time to make the prediction, as long as I didn't mind being told I was wrong, at best, or judged a fool, at worst. After all, this was the trough of the financial crisis, and the action in the market had never felt more chaotic. But once more I was confident that my investment methods allowed me to see the bigger picture.

Meanwhile, Goldman Sachs issued a research note among investors that explained why they still didn't have any faith in a rally for the financial sector.[4] Banking guru Meredith Whitney, who had become an overnight sensation for correctly forecasting the financial crisis, came out against my call on CNBC; she was also skeptical of the initial relief rally.[5] Back on TheStreet.com, Rev Shark made it a little more personal by describing my bullishness as "damn dangerous."[6]

Lo and behold, that rally wasn't just real; it was a once-in-a-lifetime opportunity that conventional wisdom just couldn't detect. My Bank of America call was subject to as much mockery as the oil call had been six months earlier, but in both cases, Alpha Hunter's David got a notch on his belt, and the traditional Wall Street Goliath took a nice black eye.

We've just discussed two of the most important investment plays of the 2007 to 2009 recession, two that very few got right. This book is going to explain the macroeconomic methodology that will help you identify future golden opportunities and position yourself to see the big picture as the market roils.

Life Outside the Box

Investment conditions on the street have undergone a paradigm shift, yet I don't think the traditionalists have noticed. They're stuck inside a box that was hammered together in the last century, and they are unwilling and unable to accept the new reality. This is especially true as you move up the ranks and into the elite analysts inside the financial institutions and among the media that keep an eye on them; they're used to dominating market perception and being applauded for their insights.

I don't trust anything I hear coming out of that old box. Investment philosophy is in critical need of a comprehensive update, even a total rewrite, and any investor who counts on his or her returns had better get up to speed, *with* speed. Most books you read won't put it that starkly, but I believe your financial future depends on recognizing that we are at a turning point in history. The courses of global markets are undergoing transformations on a scale that hasn't been seen in 100 years.

Where is the big change? It concerns the variable that was—and remains—the real market mover: confidence. The stock market acts as if the future happened yesterday; its inference of confidence in future fundamentals drives the investment strategies of the present moment.

In the twenty-first century, as digital technology pounds the world flatter and flatter, and makes us ever more dependent upon its lightning speed, we are much more susceptible to the contagious consequences of confidence or the lack of it. Worry spreads quicker than it ever did before. Momentum builds up much faster. News flow that is distributed instantaneously around the globe has dramatically enhanced the volatility of confidence.

Former Federal Reserve Chairman Alan Greenspan offered up his own insight into the new Wall Street when he said:

> After 9/11, I knew . . . that we are living in a new world—the world of a global capitalist economy—that is vastly more flexible, resilient, open, self-correcting, and fast changing than it was even a quarter century earlier.
>
> People have always been enthralled by the notion that it is possible to peer into the future. To what extent can we anticipate what lies ahead? Fortunately for policymakers, there is a degree of historical continuity in the way democratic societies and market economies

function. This enables us to reach back into the past to infer inherently persistent stabilities that, while not having the certainty we attach to physical laws, nonetheless offer a window on the future that is more certain than the random outcome of a coin toss."[7]

Greenspan was far ahead of me, and most everyone else, in noticing that we have entered a new era of investing. For me, this knowledge kicked in during a holiday conversation with Paps, just as the debacle of 2008 was coming to a close.

I start every morning the same way, by picking up the phone and calling Paps. We discuss the day's market-moving news and decide how to adjust our portfolios accordingly. None of my investment ideas pass muster until they've been hashed out during one of those morning check-ins.

Paps is my dad. He just happens to have more skepticism and common sense than any critic or advisor I've ever known. He's the man who took me under his professional wing and taught me everything he has learned in 30-plus years working as an investment advisor. He's prescient: he was investing in option LEAPS before they were known as LEAPS (you'll read about LEAPS in detail in Chapter 4). He's spent his adult life on the front lines of the market and has seen it all. So you're probably imagining his old-guy reaction when I argued that we're living on a new Wall Street. The old guys don't believe any of that rubbish. Or do they?

Me: You ready for the question of the day?

Paps: Bring it on.

Me: We all know this recessionary sell-off in 2008 has brought too many investors to their knees. How could we have helped mainstream, individual investors avoid the carnage? It didn't have to happen the way it did. So many advisors kept telling their clients to hang on and be patient through the downturn, but it kept getting worse.

Paps: I honestly think they didn't know what else to do. If you didn't get out early enough, the damage became so bad that you probably got paralyzed into inaction. The only way to crawl out of the deep hole was to stay invested at 20 percent down, then 30 percent down, and on and on.

Me: Their clients' eyes looked like deer in the headlights. Advisors love to preach the doctrine of "buy and hold," don't they? It's the only strategy most of them know. It's easy to implement, and history says it works. Buy and hold reminds me of Jerry Sloan coaching the Utah Jazz; the guy never makes adjustments, just sticks with his system no matter what. Every night he plays the same guys who run the same plays no matter who the opponent may be. Coaches like Greg Popovich and Phil Jackson love playing against the Jazz because they can make one simple adjustment and get a victory. It's inexcusable that it's been over 10 years since the Jazz won in San Antonio. In 20 years, Sloan *still* hasn't beaten Phil in a playoff series. Don't get me wrong, I'm a big fan of having a system, but there are times when you need to adapt.

Paps: Hey, watch it boy! Jerry Sloan has had a great run in Utah. Don't be so hard on him, and don't be so hard on these buy-and-holders. Until this point, the results have been in their favor. The advice they've given their clients worked in the old days, but I'll admit, in all my years in the business, I've never seen this amount of fear and volatility in the market. Many of my clients are really having a hard time with it. You've got to wonder if something has changed.

Me: You can't have an advisor like Jerry Sloan running your portfolio. Not in today's world. Buy and hold may have been the strategy of the twentieth century, but it just hasn't worked in the twenty-first century. Since 2000, investors have lived through two of the worst stock market sell-offs in history. The chase of momentum is at an extreme level. Investors need smarts. They need the ability to adapt. They can't rely on one rigid system anymore.

Paps: These two big sell-offs remind me of the saying "Fool me once, shame on you; fool me twice, shame on me."

Me: Which brings me back to my initial question. What could have been done to help out individual investors? Can you imagine what's going to happen the next time the economic cycle turns down? Investors have been burned twice in eight years. Fool me once, shame on you; fool me twice, shame on me—there won't be a third time. The next time the economic cycle turns negative, we'll see a rush to the exits. They won't let it happen a third time.

Paps: What did you just say?

Me: I said, they won't let it happen a third time.

Paps: No, before that. You said the next time the economic cycle turns.

Me: Absolutely.

Paps: Son, that's it. That is the message that individual investors need to hear. Trying to time the markets with technical analysis has never worked, which is why investors always revert back to buy and hold. But what if we can do a better job of timing the economy? Maybe a strategy built on economic timing would give investors the risk management that they're looking for.

Me: I like it. Market timing is as phony as palm reading. But economic timing—that feels more legit. I was just talking with a doctor who told me that he had wanted to get his money out of the market last year but was persuaded by his advisor to stay in. That was in February when the Dow was near 12,500. There was no reason to stay invested down to 6,600.

Paps: It's interesting that usually the average Joe recognizes we're in a recession before the financial analysts do. Every cab driver in New York City knew we were in for a rough year.

Me: We need to develop of system of economic timing that captures Main Street observations but can be proved correct by sophisticated financial analysis. It really bothers me that so many investors got duped by Wall Street when they knew exactly what was happening on Main Street.

I hung up the phone and realized that I was shocked. How could Paps be so ready to ditch buy and hold after touting its principles for his entire career? It was inconceivable that he'd join me in such a fast shift in philosophy. But the more I thought about it, the more I could see that fast or not, this was a shift brimming with common sense.

You can pull an old tradition up by its deep roots only if you have something to replace it. And whatever that something is, it needs to be better. Economic timing is better. That conversation was a game changer.

So over the next few weeks, I threw myself into creating an investment model to exploit an economic timing strategy. Paps and I extracted the best elements of market timing and combined them with the proven principles of buy-and-hold investing. We developed a Web site, the Economic Weather Station, to help investors get a feel for the new strategy. It's remarkable what two normal guys can come up with when they put their minds together. Paps and I are a poor man's Warren Buffett and his business partner, Charlie Munger. Creating a tag team that isn't afraid to talk openly and honestly about the market is a decent recipe for success and then some.

Cling to the Past at Your Peril

You can be sure that I was on my own learning curve at the time. That game changer conversation with Paps helped me identify a huge and very public mistake I'd made in the middle of the crisis, in October 2008. CNBC's Jim Cramer had appeared on NBC's *The Today Show*, and I believed that he had compounded the severe market panic by advising investors to pull out. As an adherent to the doctrine of buy and hold, I was convinced that Cramer had been reckless, not bold, and I said so on the Seeking Alpha Web site. It's worthwhile for you to read the article in full, because it's a good primer for the conventional arguments used by buy-and-holders.

Why Cramer Should Be Suspended

Financial advisors across the nation have been trying to clean up the mess that Jim Cramer made. We had clients crying because of the panic he created. Our phones have been ringing off the hook. His market call on the *Today Show* this week for investors who need funds from their accounts within five years to completely liquidate out of the stock market is the most irrational market commentary I have ever heard. At a time when a seasoned market veteran should be preaching the benefits of diversification and patience to overcome the tough times, this guy sounded more like a rookie—telling everyone to sell out after the S&P 500 had already dropped 30 percent for the year. Did he ever consider that adherence to such a strategy would collapse the entire investment system as we know it? This call might have been legitimate six months ago, but now?[8]

His irresponsibility has no right being on television. He is doing a disservice to the very people he pretends to help—the novice investor. From his platform, he has the opportunity to instill confidence in a system that is better off now than it was a year ago. Just ask Warren Buffett. We now have the $700 billion package to prop up the mortgage security market—just like Cramer said we needed. We have interest rates down to 1.5 percent—just like Cramer said we needed. On top of that we have the Fed stepping in to buy billions in commercial paper. These structural changes provide a rebuilt foundation upon which our financials can actually reap the benefits of capitalism. Capitalism doesn't work without a market. Now we have a market. And Cramer decides to bail! Over the ensuing months he must be held accountable for this one.

We've been here before with Jim Cramer. On Thanksgiving Day 2006, my dad and I made it a point to enjoy a nice bowl of applesauce in honor of Jim Cramer. Why applesauce? Because in July 2006 with Apple stock trading at its low near $50, Cramer told his viewers that they had to pull all their money out of Apple. "It's turning into applesauce, and I can't have you in it." From that very day, the stock went on to double in price over the next four months while we were invested in option LEAPS that appreciated 20 times themselves over that span. Once Cramer was out, we knew it was time to get in. Believe me, applesauce never tasted so good as it did during that Thanksgiving dinner.

There hasn't been anyone more negatively outspoken against Federal Reserve Chairman Ben Bernanke and Treasury Secretary Hank Paulson, repeatedly calling these men unsophisticated, phony, foolish, and clueless. He deserves a taste of his own medicine. It's one thing to recommend selling a stock, but it's another thing to appear on a noninvestment show—the *Today Show*—and recommend to novice investors that they should run for cover and liquidate all their capital out of the stock market. Very irresponsible. Financial suicide. Cramer should be suspended.

Empirical evidence shows that "80 percent to 90 percent of investment returns have occurred in spurts that amount to 2 percent to 7 percent of the total length of time of the holding period," says John Spears, a partner at Tweedy, Browne Company. "The rest of the time, stocks' returns have been small. You have to be in to win." Have we entered a new era of investing where this past statistic no longer matters?[9]

From 1937 to 1941, the market fell 60 percent. Since then, the two worst bear markets were 1974 to 1975 and 2000 to 2002. Both were off about 48 percent. At the intraday low last Friday, the S&P was off 50 percent from its peak last October. What kind of recovery can we expect? I think it's safe to say that historical trends will repeat themselves as they always do. $1,000 invested in the S&P 500 in 1977 left untouched would have grown to $38,730 in the 30-year period ending December 31, 2007.

However, if you would have been out of the market for the top 20 performance months out of that 360-month period, you would have only gained $6,483; costing you $32,247! Also consider a $1,000 investment made in 1998 that was left untouched through 2007 — it could have grown to $1,176. But missing only the top 20 months in that 120-month span could have cut your accumulated wealth to $498. The market moves swiftly and without warning. The risk of getting out and waiting for more stable times doesn't work because nobody knows when the big up days will come.

Today's media structure demands that commentators present new ideas every single day in order to generate ratings. This structure is not conducive to high returns. Those who try to defend Cramer's reckless call to exit the market say that he merely told people to take out the money they will need over the next five years. You really think Main Street viewers of the *Today Show* calmly got out their calculators and decided to take out that exact amount? No way. The average 401(k) investor called up his broker in a panic.

Cramer misused his credibility to lead these people into the ultimate bottom trap. He has a right to his own opinion, and I think it would have been fine to make this recommendation to a group of private clients, but it was out of line to suggest such a thing to his broad national audience. Consider the ramifications if everyone sold out of the market. Absolute chaos. He should stick to what he does best: research quality companies, recommend stocks, and promote diversification. Nobody should serve as a national market timer.

In Cramer's own words from a recent book, he says, "I have been able to make big money when big money could be made because I didn't get discouraged or fed up or desperate when times got tough. I knew that when the game eventually turned, I would be there to pounce on what was to be gained. Staying in the game makes sense rationally and empirically because, over the long term, we know stocks outperform all asset classes. The reason why more people don't get rich with stocks, though, is that people can't seem to stay in long enough to win. They get bored, tired, frustrated, defeated, or reckless. They get discouraged. They get beaten by the unnerving and jarring and humbling process not of investing but investing successfully."[10]

Buy and hold doesn't mean that we buy stocks and just bury them away. The buy-and-hold approach should focus on selecting quality companies with current market values that are at a discount relative to their underlying economic value. By accumulating these issues selectively over time and holding them, an investor minimizes transaction costs while maximizing the possibility of enjoying the long-term returns generated from the business. With the overwhelming correlation between corporate profit growth and long-term share price appreciation, there is quite a bit of wisdom in this approach. Proper asset allocation is an important part of any buy-and-hold strategy; that is the key to success, not market timing.

Points to remember:

- Historically, although past performance is not indicative of future results, a buy-and-hold strategy has resulted in higher gains over the long run.
- A big risk of market timing is missing out on the best-performing market cycles.
- Missing even a few key months can substantially affect portfolio earnings.
- Though buy and hold is a smart strategy, regular portfolio checkups are necessary.
- The time horizon is particularly important when determining asset choices.
- As goals get closer, portfolios should be rebalanced.

Only a fool throws out timeless investment principles at the top of the market and only a fool throws them out at the bottom. By deviating from the proven principle of buy and hold, Jim Cramer may look good in the short run, but his long-term success will be fleeting. Still hanging on my wall today is a picture given to me by my youth basketball coach showing a vintage "Hoosiers-like" hoop with the following phrase written below: "You miss 100 percent of the shots you don't take." My word to the wise: Don't get out of the market at these distressed levels. Remain patient. There are plenty of catalysts that will lift this market in the future. History is on your side.

Source: Seeking Alpha Web site, October 10, 2008.

Pretty persuasive, don't you think? Now I'll use the rest of this book to explain why and how that strategy became totally outdated and unreliable.

Why was I so off the mark? At the time, I hadn't noticed the increasing frequency of large sell-offs, and I didn't comprehend the reasons underlying them. It simply hadn't registered yet that history is no longer on the side of buy-and-holders. I think that article makes a credible case for the buy-and-hold strategy of the twentieth century, but the events of the last decade require more safety and flexibility in your portfolio. The hard facts show that the Nasdaq sold off from its high of 5,048 on March 10, 2000, to a low of 1,172 in October 2002, a 77 percent sell-off. If that wasn't jarring enough, we also watched the Dow drop from 14,279 on October 11, 2007, to a low of 6,440 in March 2009, good for a 55 percent sell-off. Two deep sell-offs in eight years defies any historical precedent.

So I'm sorry I came on so strong, Jim. I'll beg your forgiveness for as long as I live. I'm a passionate guy, and I'm willing to admit when I was wrong; well, that whole article was wrong.

Still Trying to Figure out a New Strategy? Catch a Wave

I grew up on the beaches of Southern California, so perhaps it's inevitable that I'll use a surfing analogy to explain buy and hold and its limitations in today's markets. Focus for a moment on Kelly Slater, who is pretty much accepted as the best surfer in his sport's history. He's a nine-time world champion as of 2009, having taken his first title at 20 and his latest at 36, quite a dominating record.

You won't see much of Slater if you hang around just one beach. According to Wikipedia, he travels all over the world to time the weather's cyclical patterns. Depending on the time of year, his favorite waves might be found at beaches in Hawaii, Florida, Barbados, South Africa, Australia, Argentina, or, of course, SoCal. He moves to where the action is best.

Now if Slater applied the buy-and-hold investment mentality to surfing, he'd sit in the water 24 hours and day, seven days a week, to be 100 percent sure he wouldn't miss the good waves. Depending on the beach he was parked at, he might have to sit in the water for a few weeks before the waves return. It's not too exciting to be sure, but it's also dangerous because the "surfer" has become a sitting duck for myriad hazards: dehydration, unman-ageable swells, sharks—you name it.

All right, so it's obvious why Kelly Slater would never sit in the water 24/7 waiting for a wave. But I'm convinced investors are just as vulnerable—and shortsighted—hanging out in the market 24/7, waiting for profits.

So why do investors do it? Proponents of buy and hold argue that since it is impossible to know when the market will make its run, it's best to stay invested always. We all know, however, that nature does not intend for us to be stagnant in a volatile climate. Buy and hold is fine under calm circumstances, but the days of calm have been replaced with days of commotion. Nowadays, getting caught in a flat-footed stance in the midst of volatility is dangerous.

Typically, the buy-and-hold argument stresses that the biggest gains occur in short periods of time. In other words, if you miss one of the big up days, you miss out on the majority of profits. In a buy-and-hold, total return strategy, $10 invested back in 1928 would have produced $17,020 by the year 2000. Buy-and-holders will point out that if you missed out on the top 30 performing months in those 72 years, you would have made only $240.

Most investment advisors love this rationale because it shows clearly and simply that buy and hold works. Why are advisors so convinced that buy and hold works best? Well, wouldn't you like to get paid to manage a buy-and-hold portfolio? It leaves plenty of time for golf, or surfing. Just wait until the market turns around. It always does.

Now I'm going to tell you the part that those advisors conveniently leave out. In the same scenario, $10 invested back in 1928 would have turned into a staggering $1,864,400 by the year 2000 if you simply had missed the 30 *worst* performance months in that time period.[11] It turns out that managing risk and getting out of the market during the worst times is the real secret to huge gains. In developing an investment strategy, it's much more important to focus on missing the worst months than it is to hit the best months. If you can accomplish both, you will be a spectacular investor. The difference between $1,864,400 and $17,020 is no small thing.

In a 1961 partnership letter, Warren Buffett described exactly this methodology when he told his partners, "I would consider a year in which we decline 15 percent and the [Dow Jones] average declines 30 percent to be much superior to a year when both we and the average advanced 20 percent." Most of us fail to grasp this investing approach and end up with inferior long-term performance relative to the benchmarks.[12]

Baby boomers were the most worshipful believers of the buy-and-hold doctrine because they grew up with and matured with the strategy. Now, as they approach retirement age, they're suffering an identity crisis. Protecting wealth, instead of growing wealth, is becoming their top priority. Ironically, they might yet discover that the two go hand-in-hand. After this decade of extreme volatility, this generation no longer trusts a market downturn. It is no longer willing to sit in the market without an understanding of the investment conditions. For years and years the statistics that described the reward of buy and hold were all anyone cared about, while the stats that illustrated the risks were overlooked. Greed for gains trumped risk management.

Well, the recent crisis has helped us to see at last that this strategy offers up a very poor attempt at risk management. In days of commotion, buy and hold is not unlike trusting a pilot who knows there is a 50 percent chance of crashing but decides to fly anyway. I wouldn't get in that plane. Accepting that level of risk is lazy, irresponsible, and unfortunately dangerous as well.

The year 2008 was even more exceptional because nobody expected much out of the stock market. Economists anticipated slower growth, a rough patch for home builders because of a much-needed correction in real estate, and an underperforming market. Most investment advisors saw the correction coming in housing, they saw that banking would be under unusual stress, and they saw the high oil prices putting pressure on profit margins for many companies, and yet they still kept their clients fully invested. Early in the year the market sent strong negative signals by selling off on both good and bad news. It was a time of minimal reward and huge risk, yet many investors stayed in the game. That doesn't make much sense at all. It's like Kelly Slater's sitting out in the ocean, with no waves, and being oblivious to weather reports screaming that there's a tsunami headed his way. That was 2008. So many investors got pummeled by the tsunami when all they had to do was get out of the water.

two

THE FOUR WINDS
OF INVESTING

Lessons of a Windsock

After a career in aerospace, my grandfather Bud kicked off "retirement" by building his own plane out in the garage. It took him years to finish, but once he was ready to take his creation out for its first flight, the whole family was keyed up in anticipation. We all went down to the local airport to witness the event.

Naturally, everyone's main concern about a homemade plane was safety. Bud showed us the different gauges in the cockpit and explained the process of coordinating with air traffic control. When I asked him about all the orange flags that were hanging around the airfield, he launched into a lecture about the brilliance and necessity of the windsock.

The windsock is designed to indicate wind direction and relative wind speed. Wind direction is the opposite of the direction in which the windsock is pointing. Wind speed is indicated by the windsock's angle relative to the mounting pole. In low winds the windsock droops; in high winds it flies horizontally. At many airports windsocks are lighted at night.

Pilots rely on instruments to help them as they take off and as they land. The wind direction and wind speed determine their flight strategy. If the wind is blowing from the west but the pilot follows his or her protocol as if it's blowing from the east, you don't want to be a passenger on that plane. A simple miscalculation in wind direction will lead to disastrous consequences. The humble windsock helps pilots avoid such disasters every day.

What an exercise in contrast that lecture was. Here I was, being introduced to a cockpit jammed with high-tech gadgetry, and simultaneously I found out that pilots still depend on something as crude and simple as a flag that blows with the wind to provide crucial information.

As you might guess, I think there is a relevant parallel between aeronautics and investing. Most investors have one set of rules that they adhere to, without regard to the current investment conditions. These rigid strategies are usually skewed for success in growing markets; even when an economy is in contraction mode, these investors think that their progrowth rules still apply. They don't.

Can you imagine what would happen to a pilot who knew how to land the plane only in a northern wind? Something as simple as an easterly wind could take the pilot out. Investors who fail to acknowledge the current "market weather conditions" expose their portfolios to unnecessary losses. A failure to implement the appropriate protocol at the right time can cause both pilots and investors to crash and burn.

William Arthur Ward tells us how to thrive in a windy market: "The pessimist complains about the wind. The optimist expects the wind to change. A leader adjusts the sails." Back in the old days wind wasn't much of an opposition. A really bad year was like 1987. That was the year of the famous Black Monday, October 19, when the Dow Jones Industrial Average fell 22.6 percent—the worst one-day percentage decline in history. Markets around the world subsequently suffered their own brutal losses. Investors were obviously shaken by the event, but in spite of Black Monday, the Dow Jones index finished the 1987 calendar year in positive territory, up 2 percent!

Investors with 401(k)s certainly had the stomach for a year like 1987. In those days it was assumed that a year in which you made only 5 percent was a bad one for the market. Fast-forward 20 years and there's no more "stomaching" a bad year. In fact, most investors have *lost* their stomachs, as if they've been riding a roller coaster gone haywire. No one can stand being at the mercy of opposition that threatens to slash your investments by 50 percent in a single year. The only way to keep standing is to identify the opposing forces and try to harness their power in your favor. To that end, let's explore the opposition through what I call the "4 winds of investing."

Wind 1: Online Trading

> *Certain winds will make men's tempers bad.*
> —George Eliot

Through the Internet, information flows instantaneously to the masses. Newspapers are struggling to survive because our society is addicted to being in the know in the now, and the Internet obliges. When the chairman of the Federal Reserve is speaking, the market is trading on his every word. When a company reports quarterly results, nobody has to wait for the analyst report to come out a few days later. It can be argued that it has long been possible to access this information so quickly, but what's certain is that it's only been in the last 15 years that a large group of people has had such immediate access. Those people are the online traders.

The Internet has transformed most every part of our society, but the investing world feels its effects more strongly than most sectors. Online trading dramatically altered the workings of the stock market. For one, the gatekeepers of the past are gone. There is no longer a broker on the other end of the phone line to calm a fearful investor who is ready to sell. As access to information has increased, professional advice has been relied on less often. More people interpret data on their own and subsequently execute their own investment strategies.

When the human interaction is less frequent, the potential for irrational anxiety increases. I think it's safe to say that this axiom applies especially to today's market. This is one of the factors that have led to increased volatility. It's no longer uncommon to see a 20 percent drop in the price of a stock within minutes. Back in the 1990s, regulators were very concerned with the unintended consequences of online trading, but after the novelty wore off and the practice became business as usual, no one gave those consequences a second thought. In 1999, SEC Chairman Arthur Levitt, Jr., issued an unprecedented warning to investors that the ease of electronic trading shouldn't blind them to its dangers: "Online investors should remember that it is just as easy, if not more, to lose money through the click of a button as to make it. . . . Retail investors should exercise caution before imitating the style of trading and risks undertaken by market professionals."[1]

Consider that in 2008, E*TRADE, one of the largest online trading platforms, added 144,000 brokerage accounts and realized over $3.5 billion in customer net asset inflows. Total retail accounts for the company numbered 4.5 million.[2] In the same year at TD AMERITRADE, the average number of trades per day reached 357,000, a rate 15 percent higher than in 2007. They opened 217,000 new accounts that brought in an additional $8 billion in assets.[3] This relatively new (and enormous) group of active traders, all with immediate access to their brokerage accounts, makes up a market dynamic that must be taken seriously.

Wind 2: Hedge Funds

> *This wind blows out candles and kindles fires.*
> —François de La Rochefoucauld

Hedge funds are the investment of choice among the wealthiest players. Originally the term *hedge fund* was meant to imply that the fund would seek to offset potential losses by hedging its investments. Reality shows that the opposite has happened in the hedge fund industry. These funds have employed strategies that have actually *increased* risk, rather than reducing it. Each hedge fund's managers feel that their strategy can outperform the market, and they are willing to take whatever risks necessary to prove it.

Hedge fund managers typically are paid a 20 percent performance fee, which creates quite an incentive to generate profits. Despite the subprime debacle, hedge fund assets have grown to more than $2.9 trillion, jumping 20 percent in the past year, according to the ninth biannual HFMWeek Hedge Fund Administrators Survey. "The movement of assets into alternatives has continued unabated despite the high fees and costs and the mixed ability of managers to deliver good performance," said Roger Urwin, global head of investment consulting at Watson Wyatt.[4]

The growth in hedge funds over the last 15 years has been exponential. Why have trillions upon trillions of dollars shifted to hedge funds as an investment vehicle? It's because wealthy, sophisticated investors are not satisfied with the average returns from the broad market. They know that the investment environment has changed, and they want to take advantage of the new volatility. So they turn their money over to hedge fund managers who are allowed to make risky bets to profit from volatility. In so doing, these funds actually create more volatility.

You rarely hear about the direct impact of hedge funds on the daily market moves, but rest assured they are always lurking under the surface of the market. Mutual fund managers are paid based on the percentage of assets they have under management, so their objective is keep those assets by generating consistent, stable returns. In contrast, hedge fund managers are paid based on a percentage of profits. They are motivated to generate high returns no matter what the circumstance. If they don't, these managers likely will face a run of redemptions as their well-heeled clients search for a better return on their investments. Goaded by this unceasing pressure, hedge fund managers manipulate and create trading positions to generate great performance over the short run even if the fundamentals don't warrant such activity. No individual hedge fund manages enough capital to move markets single-handedly, but some are definitely capable of initiating what is called a "snowball effect." If that snowball of activity starts rolling down the mountain, the results are easy to predict.

In a special report titled *The STA's Perspective on U.S. Market Structure*, the nonprofit group showed strong correlation between surges in volatility and the trading behavior of an estimated 9,000 hedge funds, many of which focus on short-term opportunities. "[This] in itself creates movement and momentum among stocks that fuels volatility and velocity," the report said, while noting that "public and private pension funds, endowments and other institutional investors have increasingly made investments in hedge funds, private equity, and other private pools of capital as a way to diversify and achieve noncorrelated returns."

Another factor linked to volatility by the STA report is the "significant increase in the number and impact of 130/30 funds," used by both traditional and hedge fund managers to enhance returns because they too involve "investment and trading strategies aimed at short-term performance."

Because they involve shorting up to 30 percent of the poor-performing stocks in a portfolio and adding weight to the best performers, 130/30 strategies typically require quick portfolio adjustments in active markets. "Algorithmic and quantitative trading models continue to increase market share," the report said, citing estimates showing that quant trading is reaching up to 50 percent of daily trading volume in some stocks and 22 percent of daily volume overall; this is because it addresses market fragmentation by seeking liquidity in multiple places.

"This results in many clients' using the same algorithms to execute orders in the same stocks. Most of the current genre of algorithms is reactive in nature." The STA report concluded: "If multiple participants use the same algorithmic trading strategies, particularly in a low volume security, the result can create a short-term price dislocation."[5]

Wind 3: Bubbles

I am always conscious of an uncomfortable sensation now
and then when the wind is blowing in the east.
—Charles Dickens

I call this the "decade of the bubble" because it has punctured no fewer than three of them. In the long run, the market does not like bubbles. They occur when the price of a particular asset class gets driven up much higher than the fundamentals warrant; it is a case of irrational momentum replacing rational investment.

During the dot-com era we watched tech stocks fly to price/earnings (P/E) multiples of 200 and above. When fund managers were questioned about investing in such lofty valuations back in 1999, they responded with a collective shrug: times had changed, that's all. They believed that these new valuations were the new norm—until they crashed, that is. The Nasdaq Index still isn't even close to half of what it was in the year 2000. The market's punishment of the dot-com bubble has lasted for nine years and counting.

After the dot-com bubble, our federal government, led by Alan Greenspan at the Federal Reserve, created an environment of low interest rates and easy lending that touched off the real estate bubble, beginning in 2004. By 2005, it was difficult to find anyone who didn't want to jump into real estate. Flipping homes had become the new fad for amateurs; unfortunately, it's always the last guys in who get burned in the bubble. After watching home prices double and triple while homeowners used their homes as a personal ATM machines through home equity lines of credit and refinancing, the amateurs rushed in, and the boom came to a crashing halt. The bursting of the real estate bubble crushed home builders and banks alike. The toxic mortgages sitting on bank balance sheets caused liquidity problems that resulted in a radical consolidation of the entire banking industry. Institutions such as Lehman Brothers, Bear Stearns, Merrill Lynch, Wachovia, Washington Mutual, and AIG either failed or were acquired in distressed takeovers. As it was (and is) for the Nasdaq in the wreckage of the dot-com bubble, it will probably take years before banking and home building stocks return to prior highs.

Then 2007 and 2008 brought the oil bubble. The oil bulls used the same arguments that we heard from tech analysts in 1999 and from real estate agents in 2005. In the midst of a bubble, any and all rationales are used to shift investor focus away from the fundamentals. With oil, it became trendy to subscribe to the "peak oil" theory, as many investment speculators felt a slowly dwindling supply would cause the price of oil to go up forever. There were a few little problems with this thesis; for starters, there were no gasoline shortages, and new oil finds were popping up around the globe. On top of that, alternative energy replacement technology was being developed that threatened the future demand for oil. Speculators conveniently looked past these potential stumbling blocks and surged ahead. Daily volumes in oil exchange-traded funds (ETFs) investments soared from 5 million in 2006 to well over 30 million in 2008. As with previous bubbles, oil's version had some nasty side effects. Consumers stopped buying SUVs because

of the high gas prices, which crippled American automotive manufacturers like GM and Ford that specialized in the high-margin,
gas-guzzling vehicles. Airlines were hammered by the rising costs.
Food prices rose in tandem with the other commodities. Many
third world countries experienced riots because of the sharply
higher prices of food. Bubbles cause a misallocation of resources
into nonoptimal uses.

But none of these troubles are greater than the fact that bubbles
burst. And when they do, the collateral damage brings many other
sectors down too. Bursting bubbles produce uncertainty, which
can paralyze the economy. Their long-term effect on the market is
rarely positive; while they elevate one sector above others, when that
sector crashes, many others are taken down with it. The bursting of
bubbles can destroy large amounts of wealth and adversely affect
spending habits.

In 2009 investors saw the beginning of the fourth phenomenon
of the decade, what I call the "uncertainty bubble." It differs
from its predecessors in that its price action is negative, but the
bubblelike characteristics that we saw in tech, housing, and
oil returned once again. Back to the axiom: once mainstream
momentum attaches itself to a cause, it will run beyond what the
fundamentals warrant.

This bubble is especially dangerous because there is nothing
investors hate more than uncertainty. So it's not hard to understand
how a bubble of uncertainty has caused a dramatic stock market
sell-off, and you can believe that, like the others, this bubble is
about to burst.

Back when the presidential campaign began, nobody knew for
certain who Barack Obama was or how he would govern. He was

inexperienced and hadn't voted his opinion very often. He was the ultimate candidate of uncertainty. This worked to his advantage in a brutal campaign during which Republicans and Democrats both were trying to distance themselves from the Bush administration.

In a weird way, this anti-Bush obsession inadvertently turned anti-American. There was a growing perception of American despair, American fear, and American greed. As a result, the majority of Americans became obsessed with finding an anti-Bush replacement, and they knew they had their man in Obama. Ironically, many people paid no attention to the details of what he said, and instead, they focused on his tremendous, articulated ability to inspire and to lead. Even moderate voters jumped on board, not because of any particular policy ideas but because they yearned for change. Let's not kid ourselves, we all know there was a tremendous "cool factor" surrounding Obama's candidacy. It was a historic moment. But the true reality of how he would govern remained a mystery.

Obama is not Bill Clinton. He is the opposite. He talks in a way that moderates can agree with, but then he governs as a liberal. Wall Street has been stunned and puzzled by this president who is more concerned with the lower and middle classes than he is about them. This situation has engendered a lot of negativity among Republicans and the conservative media, but one good thing is happening: the uncertainty from which Obama rose is dissipating. Even if you don't like how things are shaping up, it's important to remember that any plan is better than no plan.

After 2008 slouched to its miserable end, many assumed that the market could never sustain its dismal performance, but January 2009 was the worst January in history. The market dropped in 21 of Obama's first 32 days in office. Uncertainty spread from the campaign trail into the banking sector. The host of unknowns made it virtually impossible for investors to make intelligent decisions, and so the selling continued. As Warren Buffett says, in the short run the market acts as a voting machine, but in the long run it acts as a weighing machine. We all see the negative vote, but we are now at the point where another significant move down in the stock market represents the pricing in of events far worse than a recession. Our economic backs are against the wall. The bubble of uncertainty will burst as detailed solutions replace the unknown.

It's important to remember that Obama ran a flawless campaign and in office he has been very active in solving the primary problems of this crisis: banking, unemployment, and housing. It can't happen in one day, but the gradual economic healing process has begun and will soon start showing results. The market will transform from a short-term voting machine into a forward-looking, fundamentals-driven machine that is able to compare itself year over year with the 2008 recession.

With every passing quarter, those comparisons get easier. Historically speaking, the current economic fundamentals do not warrant a market sell-off of 60 percent or more. Economic history is telling us that we are in bubble territory and that the potential for a burst is very real. And the rest is history. The uncertainty was replaced with clarity, and investors cheered.

At the time when I called the peak of the bubble of uncertainty on March 6, 2009, Ford was at $1.85. GE was at $6.85. Bank of America was at $3.30. CBS was at $3.40. I wrote, "If Washington's long-term plan works to restore any form of certainty and confidence in this economy, then these stock prices represent a huge opportunity."[6] That was an understatement.

In 2009 Washington transitioned from the role of economic referee into the role of economic player, which in itself made Wall Street uncomfortable. Having a relative unknown like Obama leading the new economy has only added to market frustration. In the same way that many ignored his campaign promises, they are now ignoring the formation of his plan. Endless uncertainty will not prevail.

Investors need to understand that times have changed. This decade of bubbles has changed the investment climate of today, and it has altered the way investments should be handled in the future. Famed scientist Liberty Hyde Bailey was quoted as saying, "Every decade needs it own manual." What does the investment manual say about this decade? It says we have gone from one bubble to the next, with each burst leaving us worse off than before.

So who or what caused this short-sighted investment euphoria? You can start by looking at "Wind 2," the hedge funds. PerTrac Financial Solutions reports that over the last 10 years the number of hedge funds has increased from 600 to 13,600. Assets under management have skyrocketed from $100 billion to an estimated $2.7 trillion. Hedge funds have become mainstream in a way that was never intended. On any given day, 25 to 60 percent of global trading is handled by these unregulated funds. Knowing that each of these hedge fund managers is coping with having to produce returns of 20 percent or higher, you can see why momentum has become more indicative of future stock prices than fundamentals. These managers need quick returns, and they'll go to any length to satisfy investors. Their use of leverage, long, short, and derivative positions during volatile times has caused this decade to feel like the wild, *wild* west.

The question on investors' minds is: will we see another bubble? As long as hedge funds exert this kind of influence on world markets, you better believe we will see more momentum mania.

Wind 4: Unintended Consequences of Government Regulation

> *Beware of spitting against the wind.*
> —Friedrich Nietzsche

The fourth force working to reshape the investment landscape is not a new market dynamic; it has come out of big government, whether or not you believe "big" is a neutral description or a curse. Each round of policy change plays a significant role in the evolution of markets. I believe in free markets and capitalism's potential to stimulate the growth of our economy, but I also acknowledge that our system is heavily influenced by government regulation. Investors simply must understand the effects of those influences.

More often than not, government regulation solves the problem it was meant to fix, but in the process it creates new problems that often are not foreseen. As flawed as a world with no regulation can be, one with bad regulation often is even worse.

Everyone working in finance and investing is a champion of free enterprise. But those of us who take a long, cold look at the economy will detect that government dictates the price of beef, the crashworthiness of cars, the design of ladders, the purity of streams and air, the gender of employees, the wages of construction workers, the job prospects for teenagers, the number of lines on our television screens, the vocabulary of media entertainers, the decoration and language in the workplace, and so on. In every national crisis, the government's solutions create an entrenched constituency that prevents a return to normalcy even after the crisis has passed. As a result, each crisis leads to an increase in both the scope and scale of governmental influence, even if it has no lasting impact upon the long-term rate of the government's growth.[7]

Here are some of the latest, unintended consequences of government initiatives that are reworking the investment landscape.

Consequence 1: FASB 157

In response to the accounting fraud unearthed in the Enron scandal in 2001, new regulations were created to increase transparency for shareholders and restore investor confidence. These new laws were part of the Sarbanes-Oxley Act of 2002. This demand for increased transparency led to the most controversial new regulation of all, known as FASB 157. This new rule required banks to mark the value of their mortgage securities on a quarterly basis. At this time, housing was going through a correction, and nobody wanted to trade for a mortgage security because the underlying value of the real estate collateral was dropping. Many of these securities were built upon subprime loans that were the ugly offspring of bad lending practices, and the uncertainty surrounding their future performance kept investors away. The market for these toxic assets shut down. Nobody wanted to trade them, even though the rate of mortgage defaults was only in the single digits. As a result, our banks had to mark these securities down as low as 0.20 on the dollar in a given quarter, even though everyone knew they were more valuable than that.

But the window of time in which investors—justifiably—would be turned off by these securities was finite, and narrow. Think about fur coats in August. Nobody wants them, but it's a certainty that they'll regain their value in December. Nevertheless, the new regulation required that the banks write down all of these assets, which put their balance sheets in jeopardy of not meeting reserve requirements.

That's a very brief description of FASB 157, but I think you get the point. Regulation that was intended to create more transparency had some disastrous, unintended consequences. This regulation was officially implemented and enforced on November 15, 2007. Hmmmm. How has the stock market performed since then? Do you see any correlation?

Consequence 2: The Abolished Uptick Rule

In place for over 70 years, this rule was repealed in 2007. The SEC thought that it was out of date, unnecessary, and difficult to implement. Boy, were they wrong! This rule forces any short sale to occur at or above the last sale price on the stock. Its whole purpose is to prevent these short sellers from staging attacks on stocks. Since 2007, there have been numerous attacks on certain stocks that were completely based on rumors. In fact, this practice of "raiding" a stock became the best way for hedge funds to make money in 2008. Eddie Lampert, a hedge fund manager as well as the chairman of the board for Sears Holdings, crystallized this issue in his 2009 letter to shareholders:

Such a rule had been in place for over 70 years (to prevent "bear raids" in which short sellers aggressively sold stock at ever lower levels, undermining confidence) until it was repealed in 2007. It has been suggested that, because stocks are now traded in decimals rather than in 1/8 point increments, such a rule is obsolete or unnecessarily difficult to implement. However, what the opponents fail to point out is that companies who repurchase their own shares are advised to adhere to a rule that forbids those companies from initiating a plus tick when repurchasing shares. Why policymakers would favor an asymmetric application of a rule like this in favor of short sales and against company repurchases is a mystery.

Consequence 3: Short Selling Rules

For some unknown reason, the SEC has not been enforcing rules against what is known as "naked short selling." The term applies to short sellers who sell more shares than they actually buy, thereby manipulating pressure to the downside. The activity can be measured by the number of shares sold short, which is disclosed twice monthly by the New York Stock Exchange (NYSE) and Nasdaq, as well as by the reported tally of instances in which short sellers fail to deliver securities to purchasers of specific stocks. To anyone with common sense, this practice is ludicrous and unethical. Nevertheless, it happens. Apparently, whoever wrote the rules agreed, yet the SEC continues to be lax. As Eddie Lampert says, "The sale of property (shares) that a seller does not own and can't deliver (naked short selling) is an affront to property owners, and a destroyer of confidence and trust."[8]

Consequence 4: Nationalization of Banks

In 2008 it became obvious that the government was going to have to step in and support some of the struggling banks that were deemed "too big to fail." The government's will to act was fine; what wasn't fine was that it began taking common stock ownership in the companies. The Feds decided to run the Treasury as a hedge fund, hoping to give taxpayers a return on their investment over time as the banks recovered. What they didn't realize is that substantial government ownership in private companies limits all future growth. Private capital does not want to invest in a government-run company. The desire to help was noble, but the government's specifics of execution brought unforeseen trouble to the entire banking system. Nationalization became a precedent that injected fear into any bank that, in the future, might need governmental support. The precedent thereby killed most bank stocks. Investors don't like it when the government comes in and immediately takes away the power of management, which is exactly what it did at AIG, Bear Stearns, Freddie Mac, and Fannie Mae in 2008. Meanwhile, investors wondered: Who's going down next? Who will get saved? It became a government game of pick and choose. It was an absolute disaster of uncertainty.

The four winds of online trading, hedge funds, bubbles, and unintended consequences of government regulation have altered the market landscape so drastically that new strategies are required for success therein. Many of us have a love-hate relationship with the stock market because we have failed to adapt and accept that the wind is beyond our control. This is my chapter of great, relevant quotes so here's another, from Henry David Thoreau: "When you get out on one of those lakes in a canoe like this, you do not forget that you are completely at the mercy of the wind, and a fickle power it is. The playful waves may at any time become too rude for you in their sport, and play right over you."

Frustration and anger can't change anything. So don't get mad—get even, and adapt.

If you can learn to harness the wind by purchasing the right option LEAPS, one headed in the right direction, triple-digit returns can be yours. It's those who fail to identify the wind who will get burned. Look at all the hedge funds that were caught off guard by the oil move, by the financial move, and by the other recessionary conditions. Many of them have been forced to close their doors of operation.

The great Bob Dylan once sang, "The answer, my friend, is blowin' in the wind." (Sorry, I had to get that quote in there; I promise that's the last one!)

In *Standard & Poor's January 2009 Index Returns Report*, we see that the broad market has lost 12 percent over the last 3 years, 4 percent over the last 5 years, and 3 percent over the last 10 years. It has gained only 4 percent in 15 years and 6 percent over 20 years, but keep in mind these numbers are compounded annually and do not include taxes or inflation. Adding these factors in effectively eliminates any compounded gains over the last 20 years. The wind has indeed done some damage.[9]

If you calculate the total returns decline in S&P 500 valuation, you will find that 5 years ago the index was at 1,156, or 42 percent higher than current levels; just 10 years ago it closed at 1,224, or 55 percent higher than current levels. The Nasdaq isn't any better. In the aftermath of the dot-com burst, over $5 trillion was wiped out in market value as the technology index dropped 39 percent, 21 percent, and 32 percent in a 3-year span. To this day, that index is still 60 percent lower than it was in the year 2000.[10]

If all investors can do is come up with a buy-and-hold strategy, then their money would be much better off someplace else. It doesn't make much sense to take on the risks of investment when the rewards are so anemic. Unless an alternative to the buy-and-hold method of investing is discovered and implemented, there isn't much reason to continue putting ourselves in this precarious position. In the old days, a yearly move down 10 percent would have been considered highly volatile. Not anymore. You could come back from a vacation and find yourself down 20 percent these days.

Traditional principles of investing suggest that investors can protect themselves through diversification that incorporates their individual tolerance for risk. Unfortunately, diversification can't save you from the carnage wreaked in this new environment. All ships sink with the broad market, even the so-called defensive stocks or dividend payers. Year-over-year performance on the S&P 500 dividend-paying ETF was negative 54 percent in 2008.

For most investors, limiting downside risk is their number 1 priority. Its importance far outweighs the expectation of high returns. I receive more client phone calls when the market is down 500 points then when it's up 500 points. In fact, the phone never rings on days when the market is up. An investment portfolio is an accumulation of hard-earned money that is supposed to provide you with a nice nest egg for retirement. Return of capital is essential, even if it means generating a little less return on capital.

The primacy of the buy-and-hold strategy needs to be reexamined. I don't say this lightly; I know many readers will read those words and be immediately hot for a fight. But if you're hot under the collar right now, please try to hold your reaction in for a moment. I want you to consider a foundational truth about the stock market. It's not some unchanging, unalterable institution that has been here since the beginning of time and will be here until the end of time. Sometimes we fool ourselves into believing that the market is a kind of religion and that there's only one, orthodox method of worship. Actually, the rules for success within the stock market can change, they do change, and they have changed.

The cold, hard facts of this decade's poor performance merely affirm what most of us have felt for some time: our world and the markets within it are experiencing a new era of extremism. It's true that this extremism can cause wonderful short-term gains to the upside, but over the long run the overall market does not perform well because of the increased volatility. Volatility brings many unintended consequences. Downside volatility leads to uncertainty and fear, which both erode the confidence of our stock market and our economic system.

If there's one thing you never want to mess with, it's the confidence of an economy. Scholars have debated the causes of the Great Depression for the last 70 years. Most of these debates circle around a specific policy that was or wasn't enacted during the 1920s and 1930s; in all those years, little consensus has been established. Except for one fact: everyone agrees that a loss of consumer confidence is what finally threw the economy over the cliff. In our own era of volatility, this same loss of confidence carries no less threat than it did 70 years ago. It's like the old Green Bay Packers coach Vince Lombardi once said: "Confidence is contagious. So is lack of confidence."

Investor anxiety reminds me of a story about an elevator. A white woman arrived in Los Angeles for a business trip during the LA race riots of 1989. The uproar left her feeling very nervous and concerned for her safety. After checking in at the front desk of her hotel, she headed to the elevator. She quickly entered, and when she looked up, she saw three black men already inside. Her tremors started in again, but she told herself, "This is ridiculous, I have nothing to fear from these men, here in the middle of a reputable hotel. OK, no problem, I'm going to ride this elevator, etc. . . . ." Shortly after the elevator door closed, one of the men said, "Hit the floor, lady." She immediately dropped to her stomach in terror. The three men broke out into hysterical laughter. The speaker simply had meant for her to *press the button for her floor.*

She was terribly shaken and embarrassed, but she had her business to attend to and so tried to forget about the incident. At the end of her stay, when she went to check out, she was bewildered when the clerk informed her that her bill had been paid for. He then handed her a note that had been left by the person who had picked up her tab. It read:

> *Thanks for the best laugh I've ever had in an elevator.*
> —**Eddie Murphy**[11]

Uncertainty creates risk. Taking an uncomfortable risk causes some of us to lose sleep and causes others to distort common sense. Putting yourself in a circumstance beyond your acceptable tolerance for risk can cause you to lose your mind just like the lady in the elevator.

Investors can't afford to lose their minds. They might sell out of the market at the worst possible time, or they might buy something covered in warning labels. Whether your investment profile in conservative, moderate, or aggressive, you need to know how comfortable or uncomfortable you are when the value of your investment moves up or down. All investments carry risk, but some are more risky than others.

I know I've already broken my promise to stop quoting, but nobody understood the unpredictability of the wind like Thoreau, so let's wrap with one last glimmer of his wisdom: "There is the power of the wind, constantly exerted over the globe. . . . Here is an almost incalculable power at our disposal, yet how trifling the use we make of it! It only serves to turn a few mills, blow a few vessels across the ocean, and a few trivial ends besides. What a poor compliment we do pay to our indefatigable and energetic servant!" Alpha hunters understand the elements around us, and use them to our benefit.

three

ECONOMIC TIMING

An Investor for All Seasons

One of my favorite vacation destinations is the Snowbird Ski Resort. Utah is known for having the greatest snow on earth, and this resort, nestled in God's snowmaking factory, Little Cottonwood Canyon, gets the best of the best powder. *Skiing* magazine named Snowbird the number 1 ski resort in the United States for five years in a row. With its runs among the steepest and the most challenging, this is a winter wonderland for enthusiasts.

I book my room at the Snowbird Lodge for the same weekend every year because I know that's when the conditions will be just what I'm looking for. I show up at Snowbird right around the Fourth of July. Wait, you say; was that a major typo? Is this guy some sort of extreme gravel skier, or hasn't he mastered the Gregorian calendar yet?

None of the above. Let me explain. The seasonal transformations at Snowbird are the most dramatic I have ever witnessed.

The raves about its deep winter powder aren't hype, but I assure you that its summer beauty is just as majestic. The fresh mountain air somehow reinvigorates the lungs, and the visual display of nature soothes the mind. When my family and friends gather there, the kids love playing in the mountain playground, we race down the Alpine slide, the bravest head down the zipline, others ride the Tram and hike the mountaintops, and then we all meet up poolside for the most relaxing hot tub hangout on planet Earth. The summer at Snowbird reminds me of what freedom really is; I wouldn't celebrate Independence Day anywhere else.

If summer in the mountains isn't your thing, try the autumn. The fall colors at Snowbird are so vibrant that it's hard to believe the spectacle is even real. An odd human tendency is our need to identify our "routine favorites" and then stick to them. Snowbird helps me to break free of that tendency. It's my hope that reading this chapter will help you to do the same.

Rigid complacency can do a lot worse than keep the beauty of Snowbird chained to a pair of skis. It can also crush your investment portfolio. Identifying and adapting to the different cycles of the economy is the guiding principle of successful investment management. This principle informed Warren Buffett when he coined an oft-repeated investment slogan: "Buy when others are fearful, and sell when others are greedy." Buffett understands that the only constant in life is change.

Look at all of the cyclical examples nature has given us to learn from. On a daily basis we travel along the cycle of exertion and rest. The circumstances of our lives are the product of cyclical development, from birth to old age. A butterfly starts out as an egg, hatches into a caterpillar, changes into a chrysalis, and then emerges as the winged butterfly. Some cycles dwarf human existence, such as seasonal weather, the daily ocean tides, and the rotation of the planet itself.

Our adaptation to cycles is often ingrained deeper than consciousness. We don't have to be told not to wear flip-flops and shorts in the ice and snow. I don't wait to buy my bat and glove until the end of baseball season. Other preparations for coming cycles aren't automatic, yet they too are essential. Perhaps many of us still believe there really is no beating the economic cycle of prosperity followed by misfortune, but I believe you can stay ahead of the curve and profit from both. Don't let human nature convince you that you can enjoy Snowbird only in the winter. Become a man or a woman for all seasons.

Many investors have been so burned by bad strategy that they have lost all hope for consistent solutions. To them, the market feels like a chaotic storm that moves without rhyme or reason. That perspective is easy to fall into, and once you're there, it is hard to climb out. To those who may be in such a state, I have an important insight to share with you: cycles are easy to detect *as long as you know to look for them*. The stock market sends out signals that are just as obvious as the setting sun presaging the night. You need only pay attention.

Reflecting on the last 20 years of anemic returns should be enough to get us to adopt a better way to produce high returns in our portfolios. One better way would have been simply to avoid the market during recessions.

Did you know that 90 percent of amateur pilots fly only in good weather? On days they're scheduled to fly, they pore over the weather report with keen interest before taking off. These pilots aren't instrument rated, they wouldn't know what to do in a dense fog or in a heavy storm, so wisely they refuse to take the risk. Why isn't it the same in the stock market? Why aren't investors looking to the "economic weather report" to determine their strategy? For most individual investors, the way to survive and flourish in this era of volatility is to invest only in good conditions. Unless an investor considers himself or herself "instrument rated," capable of navigating even tempests, there is a strong case to be made that he or she would be crazy to be in the market 100 percent of the time.

It's the Rate of Change

Now it's time to discuss economic timing and its benefits. How do the returns compare to buy and hold? The only dates that I am interested in testing against are post-January 1, 2000. Buy and hold worked just fine before that date, but since then its followers have gotten slammed.

Since January 1, 2000, compounded annualized returns using my system of economic timing turned $100,000 invested in the Dow Jones Industrial index into $162,944, representing a very healthy 62.9 percent gain. If you had simply stayed in the market that entire time, adhering to the buy-and-hold strategy, your $100,000 would have turned into $76,023—a 24 percent total loss. Economic timers are more than twice as wealthy as buy-and-holders since 2000. (This data was calculated in June 2009.)

So what exactly is economic timing? There are certain data measurements within the economy that do a great job of identifying its current condition. When these indicators tell us that the economy is improving, it is time to be invested. When those indicators tell us that the economy is worsening, it is time to sell out. Economic timing takes a macroeconomic approach to determining the cycles of the stock market.

If the economy is improving, it doesn't necessarily mean that the key data points are in positive territory. Improvement is indicated by a positive *rate of change* between prior releases of the data and the present calculation. Rate of change is your new best friend. The rate of change can accelerate at an increasing rate, or it can decelerate but at a decreasing rate; in other words, the rate of change is slower or faster than it was before.

Investors should never look at a growing economy and think it's time to abandon the prudent practice of asset allocation or diversification. They can, however, use such indicators to infer that the downside risks are limited. When these indicators tell us that the economy is in decline or isn't growing as fast as it once was, it is time to be cautious and go into a defensive portfolio strategy. I will outline portfolio strategies for both an improving economy as well as a worsening economy in Chapter 4.

The moves in and out of the market in an economic timing strategy are much less frequent than with technical analysis, and they are more proactive than with a buy-and-hold strategy; it strikes a happy medium between the two. Patience is an essential virtue of investing, but you want to be sure your patience will pay off. Ask yourself why, when no one expected 2008 to be a great year for the stock market, so many people stayed invested throughout it? To what end? The risk was huge and the reward was so small. Economic timing is designed to keep clear of exactly this type of situation.

The stock market always looks forward. That is why stocks react to the direction of the data rather than to the position of the data.

It's critical that this point be perfectly clear: even when the data is negative, the stock market can still be a great place to invest if the *rate of change* of the data is showing marginal improvement. History shows us that the stock market typically recovers before the economy does. Why does this happen? It's because the future direction of the economy determines the price action. Every quarter, the results of publicly held companies are compared to their results of the previous year. These comparables get easier to match the deeper the economy gets into a recessionary environment. This is why growth rates tend to surge when an economy begins its recovery mode; the comparables are very favorable. The opposite also holds true: when the economy has been roaring along year after year, comparables become difficult to match. Our focus on the rate of change of growth is so profitable because it helps us gauge the probability that stocks will either surpass or fail previous comparables.

Every investor needs to come up with a system that frames the "big picture." We can all get lost in the trees to the point that we no longer see the forest; so many variables affect stock market pricing that it's difficult to consider them all without a system. Every smart investor, unless he or she is some kind of savant, employs a comprehensive system that monitors the critical variables.

Ten Weather Tips to Start With

Before I ever make an investment decision, I make sure to check the economic weather. Which way is the economic wind blowing? Which way are my stocks blowing? In order to know the direction of the economic wind, there are several economic data points that need to be monitored. Many investors are tripped up because they focus on too few of them. History has shown us that the following economic data points serve as an accurate indication of economic direction.

GDP

As Investopedia says, the gross domestic product is the Godfather of the economic indicator world. It measures total economic production for a country by representing the market value of all goods and services produced by the economy during the period measured, including personal consumption, government purchases, private inventories, construction costs, and foreign trade balance. In the United States, we get an advanced release four weeks after the quarter ends and a final release three months after the quarter ends. We consider 2 to 3 percent growth per year to be moderate growth, and we define a recession as two consecutive quarters of negative growth.

If you were forced to use only one economic indicator this would be the one. It's the one that frames the big picture, and it gets your forecast started in the right direction. That said, I'm not recommending you rely on it exclusively: the weakness of this data is that it isn't very timely.[1]

Mutual Fund Flows

I love this indicator because it is a true gauge of market sentiment. The Investment Company Institute and the AMG Database of Fund Flows & Holdings serve as reliable sources of money flow trends. The metric is presented as a total amount of inflows or outflows. Observing the rate of change of this data point does a good job of identifying the velocity of the market in terms of supply and demand.

In the last few years ETFs have been taking money from the mutual fund industry, so it is a good idea to track both. Weekly readings are irrelevant, but multiple data points indicate a trend and serve as a valuable resource to confirm the economic direction.[2]

Employment Data

Employment data can be gathered from a mixture of the weekly jobless claims report and the monthly release of the national unemployment rate. The weekly report shows the number of filings for state jobless claims around the nation. It takes into account the seasonal effect on hiring, so you don't need to be worried about things like a huge dip in unemployment right after the holiday shopping season.

The most important indication you can derive from employment data is that when you have more employed workers, there will be more disposable income and personal consumption being injected into the economy. However, employment data is referred to as a "lagging indicator" because as a general rule, companies will hold on to their workers as long as possible before cutting jobs. In fact, because layoffs are so traumatic to a company, most of them hold on to their workers longer than they should during rough times. By the time the cycle improves, they are slow to hire because they remain gun shy from having endured the weak growth cycle. They always seem to be one step behind.

Despite its being a lagging indicator, I still include it in my overall economic barometer because the weekly number gives a real-time view of what is happening, and it also projects a major part of the economy.[3]

Inflation

Inflation is measured from two perspectives, the consumer side and the producer side. Consumer inflation is measured by the consumer price index (CPI), which factors in the prices of a basket of goods typically used by consumers on a daily basis, such as milk, eggs, and toothpaste. The Bureau of Labor Statistics releases the CPI once a month, usually at the midpoint. The Fed likes to see the CPI within their target range, which depends on the economic environment and thus is subject to change; you need to pay attention to what the Fed has to say when it releases the minutes of its regular meetings. One of their principal jobs is to manage inflation by cutting or hiking interest rates.[4]

The Bureau of Labor Statistics also produces a monthly report on producer price inflation (PPI). This is a weighted index of prices measured at the wholesale and/or producer level. All physical goods that are produced in the U.S. economy are included. The PPI is usually released a few days in advance of the CPI, and it does a good job of alerting investors to initial signs of inflation before its spreads to consumers.

Consumer Confidence

The Conference Board, a nongovernmental organization, and the University of Michigan both release monthly consumer confidence reports. They're gathered through the use of telephone surveys conducted within samples of the United States to determine consumer attitudes toward the business climate, personal finance, and spending.[5] While it includes no hard data, this economic data point does a great job of forecasting future spending and saving behavior. Market psychology is a major influence on stock prices, and these consumer sentiment reports offer a glimpse into the consumer's mind. Consumer expectations are focused on how they view prospects for their own financial situation and for the general economy over the near term and long term. Consumer spending forms the lion's share of the GDP, usually accounting for 40 to 70 percent of it.

In the midst of a downturn, why does the stock market typically recover before the economy does? Shouldn't we have to wait for employment to improve or for GDP to turn positive? Well, despite how handy that syllogism would be if it were true, that just isn't the way things work. The market recovers before the economy because *confidence* is the real driver of the market, and confidence can be restored before the data improves. Confidence trumps most other economic data, it trumps technical analysis, and it trumps corporate earnings. Without confidence, a sense of despair looms over the market and turns it into a sea of negativity that swallows up any sign of good news.

The perfect case study is the financial crisis of 2008. Rewind the tape to the end of September, and you'll hear President Bush neatly summarize the propaganda of fear that was in everyone's ears. "Failing to act fast risks wiping out retirement savings, rising foreclosures, lost jobs, closed businesses, and even a long and painful recession," he said.[6] His dire warning caused the mark-to-market balance sheet debacle of Wall Street to incite panic on Main Street. This was a severe mistake. Instead of confining Wall Street's problems to Wall Street, Bush's administration got the entire nation involved. The tactic of using fear to drive policy brings unintended, often perilous consequences.

When we actively imagine future trouble and despair, we can be articulating a self-fulfilling prophecy. I'll never forget hearing

CNBC's Maria Bartiromo say in an April 2008 interview with Tim Russert, "We could be talking ourselves into a recession . . . because of all of the headlines and all of the negativity out there."[7] But really, how often does confidence take a world-class beating? Not very. When it does, it creates a rare, ripe opportunity for those who can identify its return.

To those economists who argue against the fundamental impact of stimulus, I would say, "You don't understand the necessity of confidence." Anything that restores confidence during uncertain times is positive, and the fact that these confidence-enabling events aren't going to happen tomorrow is actually a good thing. If they occur too quickly, when panic is still in the atmosphere, the goodwill and steadiness they can provide likely will come and go in the same day.

Currency

Two years ago Paps met with a group of Italian investors who described a very dark economic landscape across the European continent. The landscape hasn't gotten much sunnier of late. The weak dollar has taken its toll on overseas tourism. Italy, France, Spain, Germany, and the United Kingdom cannot handle another slow travel season. Look for governments abroad to do all they can to decrease the value of their own currencies; otherwise, they may well find themselves headed toward depression. The United States, on the other hand, would prefer that the dollar remain low as profits abroad offset weakness at home, but the Treasury knows it can sustain these conditions for only a season, and that season is about to end.

With Europe's back against the wall, the currency landscape is about to change. We have grown accustomed to low domestic stock price valuations brought on by the weak dollar. Even as our economy experienced its latest boom from 2003 to 2007, P/E ratios remained tame. The 10-year return on the S&P 500 prior to the recession was a meager 3.5 percent, compared with 6.84 percent on the European 350 Index and 12.27 percent on the MSCI Emerging Markets Index. The only way to get decent multiples on our stocks is to have international demand. Why haven't we had international demand? It has had nothing to do with economic performance and everything to do with currency. Even if our Italian friends had made all the right U.S. investment moves over the last five years, they still would have lost money because of exchange rates.

Don't be naive to the influence of currency valuation on the stock market. The prediction of tomorrow's strong dollar can cause a major relocation of worldwide assets today. International demand is enhanced when currency is favorable. It will be interesting to watch how the international community deals with the U.S. dollar in the future. Countries such as China and Russia have been vocal in their concerns about the impact inflation might have on the dollar. Their concerns are so profound that they are rumored to be looking to get away from the dollar as their reserve currency and diversify into the International Monetary Fund (IMF). It's still unlikely that we'll see anyone make such a drastic move because the residual damage would be massive—not just in this country but in any country with an economy closely linked to ours. But the fact that such a move is even discussed makes this a story worth watching. If demand for dollars ever dries up, it will be difficult for the stock market to overcome the currency weakness.[8]

Leading Economic Indicators

This economic data point historically changes direction before the economy does. The leading indicators are reported by the Conference Board, which determines the value of the leading indicator index from the values of 10 key variables. These variables have historically turned downward before a recession and upward before an economic expansion. The 10 components of the index include the following: initial applications for unemployment insurance, manufacturers' new orders for consumer goods and materials, speed of delivery to vendors from suppliers, nondefense capital goods orders, new building permits for residential building, the S&P 500 Index, inflation-adjusted money supply (M2), spread between long and short interest rates, consumer sentiment, and average weekly hours worked by manufacturing workers.[9]

Investors should never focus solely on this economic data point because, while it has indeed forecasted each recession we've had since 1959, it also predicted five others that never occurred. Referring to this mixed record, economist Paul Samuelson once said, "Economists have correctly predicted nine of the last five recessions."

Retail Sales

The Census Bureau and the Department of Commerce release U.S. retail sales in another midmonthly report, which covers the immediately previous month. Year-over-year comparisons are the best way to track this data because it reflects seasonality. In calculating the rate of change, you should look at the sequential rate of changes based on the year-over-year numbers; don't just calculate sequential data. As I mentioned, consumer spending makes up a large chunk of the GDP, so any extended drop-offs in this data point can indicate coming danger. I especially like the retail sales indicator because it is released monthly, instead of quarterly like the GDP and corporate earnings reports are released.[10]

Corporate Revenue

Corporate revenue growth is the most trusted data point I know of because there is no way anyone can manipulate it or hide from it. Revenue is reported as the amount of money that a company receives during each quarter. This is the total amount of money brought into the company from its business activities. Earnings (or net income) are not as impressive to me because they are dependent upon management's effectiveness. Net income is important when choosing a company to invest in, but it doesn't help us when trying to identify the overall health of the economy.

Unfortunately, there is no official report that I know of to tell you exact growth rate numbers for widespread corporate revenue. But if you pay attention, you can usually search for the topic and find some good summary articles after the earnings season ends each quarter.

Earnings Estimates

I do not pay attention to earnings estimates that come from the companies themselves because the forecasts that they provide have severe conflicts of interest. It is in the best interest of companies to temper future expectations so that their actual performance will meet or beat the benchmarks. Hence, the earnings estimates that come directly from the companies are often a means to game managing expectations instead of a means to provide informative, trusted indicators.

The indicator that I like comes from the earnings estimates of analysts. These are the folks who track most stocks and supposedly have a good handle on the future of the individual companies. After all, that's their full-time job. I have a hard time trusting analysts on individual stocks, but I have found that the collected analyst opinion can be a helpful indicator. When you hear about mass analyst downgrades, there is usually a fundamental reason why. It's possible they've latched on to a fad indicator that our other nine economic indicators don't track yet but that is still capable of giving useful information about the market.

Although there isn't a sure-fire way of tracking changes to analysts' earnings estimates, you can follow them in your daily searches. Put all of those Wall Street analysts to work for you. Just be careful not to follow their advice blindly. All too often, analysts are more concerned with their own reputation than they are with making the right call. If a stock has dropped too much, the analyst will lower his or her rating so that he or she appears more in line with reality. This practice does everyone else a bad turn; good investing is all about buying low and selling high. If you follow the analyst who has jiggered his or her rating for the sake of appearances, you might end up selling low and buying high. Know what you're dealing with on this one.

Those are my 10 economic indicators. Just as the Federal Reserve has levels of acceptable rates of inflation, I have levels of acceptable rates of change for the data. I recommend you use a moving average of the previous four readings of data. If you are tracking retail sales, there may be a month-to-month reading that doesn't fit with the trend. This is normal and shouldn't cause you alarm, unless you begin to see the same pattern emerge in another economic variable or if more than one month bucks the trend. Be careful not to formulate a new investment thesis based on only one reading. By tracking at least 10 economic variables, you won't get head-faked into making drastic decisions.

Remember that economic timing is a more calculated hybrid of the buy-and-hold strategy and the tendency toward high-frequency trades in and out of the market. Economic timing wants you ready to move or stand pat depending on what your rate-of-change comparisons are telling you. It's meant to prepare you to handle the market during the good years and the bad years alike. The more reliable you can make your rate-of-change comparisons, the better view you will have of the economy.

Every once in a while a different piece of economic data will come along that consumes the market's attention. In such times, that particular piece of data should be added to the 10 indicators I listed above. For instance, housing was a hot piece of data during the last recession, and so I added it into my track pad during 2008 and 2009. There will be times when bond yields are hot enough to track. When that happens, make sure your track pad is up to date.

It is also important to keep detailed reports of these 10 economic indicators. Each time new data is released, it should be compared with the previous results. In my personal investment log, which I'll open up in a later chapter, I like to have an updated arrow affixed to each category that indicates if the rate of change is improving or worsening. An up arrow means either that the rate of change is increasing at an increasing rate, or that the data is decreasing but at a decreasing rate as to what it was before. A down arrow means that the rate of change is increasing at a decreasing rate or it is decreasing at an increasing rate of change.

The economic timing investment strategy, based on rate of change, is designed to be anticipatory of market action rather than reactionary. It also needs to combine sequential economic data with year-over-year data to provide a more accurate view of the current conditions. A sophisticated understanding of the rates of change among these various economic data points will create your own personal investment barometer.

As I mentioned earlier, the problem with most investors is that they have only one set of rules. Or in pilot speak, they know how to land a plane only when the wind is blowing in one direction. Economic timing opens your eyes to the various market environments, and as such, it requires different strategies for the different market conditions. When you are prepared for a downturn, you will experience far less stress than you will have if you get blindsided. And your portfolio can be kept safe and secure despite the volatile conditions.

While the media and analysts love to chew on the past, successful investors are already five steps ahead, forecasting the future direction of the market. All those talking heads are distracting, so much so that investors get caught up in the chatter and keep losing their money instead of trying to predict what's coming next. How can it be that Google (GOOG) reports an unbelievably great quarter but its stock sells off? How can Google report a subpar quarter only to see its stock surge? It's all because of the expectation for future performance. Investors are leery about being part of a declining growth story.

Catching the Trends the Analysts Miss

This tug-of-war between the past and the future is in full swing as the overall economic direction shifts. As you near the end of a recession and approach a recovery, all the worst readings of the economic data will pop up. Corporate revenue growth, unemployment, and GDP will be horrendous, and most will interpret this as the preface to the next leg down in the stock market. A cynical mindset would tell you that the stock market should tank in such an environment, but will it? Not if the data is slowing enough to suggest a coming turn. Around the coming corner, the comparisons with the previous year will be more favorable, and growth will come more easily.

At the beginning of an economic downturn the stock market feels like a war zone that gets more dangerous with the release of each economic data point; any one of them could represent a minefield because the comparables and the expectations are so difficult to beat. In the early months of 2008, employment reports were met with huge sell-offs, even though the data in and of itself wasn't that bad; in fact, it was still positive, but the market didn't care. Its rate of change was worsening. The same thing happened during earnings season as decent earnings reports were sold down; even those companies that were improving their rates of growth saw their stocks sell off as good news was interpreted as bad news. Those who were long the market were endlessly frustrated by the market's negative interpretation of the positive data. That was 2008. It was a year of premature bottom calls as too many investors allowed anxiety to get the best of them. Emotional optimism jumped in front of numeric reality.

In 2009, it's been the opposite. The unemployment rate reached its worst reading in 25 years at 9.5 percent and the market went up on the news! You should have seen some of the guests on CNBC when that happened. They had no clue why the market was going up. They didn't understand it. Those guys are old Wall Street. Apple reported that February Mac and iPod sales were down 20 percent year over year. It was the first year-over-year decline in at least five years, but the stock still climbed from $80 to $115.

In 2009 bad news is treated as if it were good news. The only thing that matters is rate of change. Many in the media like to use the metaphor of a green shoot to illustrate this behavior. Green shoots are the fledgling signs of new life. The technical term for tracking green shoots—that is, the rates of change of various data points—is *second derivative*. It is a calculus term that describes the basis for my economic timing model, and as such I have to defend it. Calculus scares everyone off, and it's a far more complex system than we need here. What you need to know is that if the directional velocity is showing that the worst is behind us, stocks will begin the process of pricing in the future. The year 2009 was the year of premature top calls, as the majority of investors don't believe in the rally because it isn't supported by strong growth. But it doesn't need strong growth. It only needs to show a change in direction, and the market will recover before the economy does.

Technical analysis doesn't catch these kinds of trends. Technical analysis is a method of market timing that seeks to utilize indicators such as buy signals, hold signals, and sell signals to interpret the wavelike movements of the markets. Trading is much more frequent than it is with buy and hold, so investors must factor in higher trading costs and tax bills. Market timing may help you dodge deep declines, but it's riskier when it's time to determine when to get back in for the big turnaround. Its charts usually don't show good set-ups until the big gains have been had.

So we have another reason why so many have stuck with buy and hold: technical analysis is worse. It is a controversial strategy that is open to diverse myths and interpretations. Sometimes I'll see the screen of a technical analysis trader and wonder what on earth he is looking at. It looks more like a page out of an astrology textbook than an investing textbook. These guys try to forecast the future direction of daily prices based on charts of current price and volume, but they ignore the actual fundamentals of the market. It's the polar opposite of buy and hold.

The primary reason you can end up in trouble with a market timing service is that a directional compass isn't enough. Remember the *Titanic*? The "unsinkable" ship, the one that was zooming across the Atlantic on its maiden voyage in 1912, right on course, at an impressive (for the time) 22½ knots? A technical marvel of its time, it still couldn't avoid the iceberg in its path. Belief in the "unsinkable" fallacy doomed over 1,500 people, as there were only enough lifeboats for half of those on board.[11]

Fortunately, nautical engineers learned from *Titanic*'s sinking. Modern boats are equipped with a GPS system as well as radar to detect obstructions in their path, and they have lifeboats for everyone. Now back to investing: to suggest that independent price movements and volume can tell you which stocks to buy and when to buy them is thinking like the builders of *Titanic*. I can't tell you how many times I have heard technical analysts calling for a rally or a bottom that never came in 2008. They thought that their technical indicators could overcome the financial crisis and could navigate through declining unemployment and all the other fundamental data that was in decline, but they couldn't. Extreme behavior is not built into many of their models, and we happen to live in a new world that is dominated by extreme behavior.

The two strategies of buy and hold and technical analysis have their moments of effectiveness, but neither is ideally modeled to take advantage of the market we have lived with since 2000. There is no reason to be married to one or the other. Economic timing takes the best of both strategies. It times the market over the long run, which still allows investors to experience the benefits of buy and hold without the negative risk of blindly staying invested. The economic timing model clearly identifies the various cycles of the market with its second derivative, economic indicator approach.

A vital step to becoming an alpha hunter is to know what you are hunting, and in what season. I might be against the grain enough to go to Snowbird in July, but I'm not dumb enough to bring my ski equipment. Economic timing is the weather report for the market that sets you up for your next big decision: what investment tools do you need to utilize in order to take advantage of the conditions and achieve alpha performance?

A thorough catalog of the necessary tools will require another chapter; for now, we'll start with the most basic, which is less a tool than it is a position. You need to find the high ground.

I'm not about to suggest investing is any sort of equivalent to warfare, but in fact generals throughout history have known, better than most of us, the value of gaining command of the high ground, both because it's the most secure and because it allows them the best view of what's happening in the field.

Consider the Allied armed forces who landed on the Normandy beaches on June 6, 1944, D Day. American troops, along with soldiers from five other nations, sustained terrible casualties as they crawled off the beaches and up to the higher elevations occupied by German defenses. In some cases, the "elevation" amounted to little more than a few feet, yet it amounted to a foothold in Western Europe, and the Allied commanders knew it was worth the high price they paid. [12]

In our more peaceful times, economic timing keeps you on the high ground of the stock market. It doesn't mean that the battle is over or even that victory is assured. But it is a crucial step to finding success.

four

NAVIGATING WITH LEAPS

The Optimal Investment Tool

Using the resources of economic timing, you will find the high ground; now it's time to select your best weapon. This requires a little honest introspection on your part.

I'll start with some painful confessions. No matter how hard I try, I cannot paint like Picasso. I was not granted his artistic gifts, to say the least. At my school, eighth-grade art was a mandatory elective. After our first project I went up to my teacher and asked if she would grant me an exemption and allow me to take woodshop a second time. Would she let me, a student, buck the system? She didn't even think twice. I was out.

The best sound system in the world won't make me sound like Pavarotti. In ninth grade the music director put out an open call for any and all males who wanted to join the choir. My buddy and I jumped at the opportunity because it meant a free trip on the choir's upcoming tour with some girls we liked. When I tried out, the director said, in the best Broadway tradition, "We'll call you." They didn't.

It's idealistic and perhaps good-hearted to believe that any of us can become whatever we want in this life. But it's far better to take time and discover your own unique gifts and develop them instead of trying to compete when you lack the basic tools. If you're five feet tall, there is no chance of becoming an NBA center. Don't fight it; just find your own thing. I've been around many people who have chosen to pursue careers they weren't equipped to master, and all the while they ignored gifts that would have brought them great satisfaction if they had followed another path. We are all different, and there's no reason to covet the gifts of another; instead, we should celebrate our own and focus on developing our skill with tools that suit us.

When it comes to investing, I don't think there's a tool better suited to today's volatility than options. Options are more gifted than stocks. Option calls and option puts will position you to navigate the prevailing market weather conditions. As it is with people, dealing with the gifted investing tools can be both a joy and a frustration. To understand why, you need to realize that being gifted is not a measure of performance; it is merely of measure of innate ability.[1] We have incentive to stick with options not because of their innate ability but because when they do perform correctly, they can make us very wealthy.

Options are derivatives, not to be confused with the calculus terminology of "second derivatives" that we discussed in the previous chapter. These are completely different. Derivatives are financial contracts or financial instruments whose values are derived from the values of their underlying assets. You can trade derivatives in commodities, equities, mortgages, commercial real estate, loans, bonds, interest rates, exchange rates, inflation, weather conditions—you name it and you can probably find a derivative to invest in.

The term *derivative* has gained a negative connotation through the financial crisis because many of the credit swaps and mortgage derivatives lost their value at accelerated rates and led to panic at the banks that owned so many of them. So are they good, or are they evil? The answer is that it depends on how they're used. When derivatives are used in illiquid markets, and when speculators utilize high ratios of leverage or margin (debt) to purchase these contracts, they are very bad. As Warren Buffett says, "These highly complex financial instruments are time bombs and financial weapons of mass destructions that could harm not only buyers and sellers but the whole economic system."[2]

But used in the proper environment, derivatives are the best way to invest. The same guy who called derivatives "weapons of mass destruction" doesn't think they're guaranteed to blow up in his face. His Berkshire Hathaway investments currently hold several dozen derivative positions such as futures and options contracts on stock indexes and foreign currencies. And as a matter of fact, Buffett has also stated publicly that all "derivatives aren't evil." At his annual shareholders' meeting in May 2009, he announced that he had doubled down on his position in S&P 500 options by extending the time horizon on these contracts out to near 2020.

There are right and wrong ways to invest in derivatives. Don't do what the banks did. Do what Warren Buffett does. He invests in derivatives that are assured of maintaining a market for liquidity, he doesn't invest in short-term options, and all of his speculative plays are long-term options.

The best kind of derivatives are options, and the best kind of options are called Long-Term Equity Anticipation Securities, or LEAPS. The mainstream use of options has exploded in recent years because they offer stock investors so much more versatility in their portfolios. Options are touted as one of the most successful financial products to be introduced in the most recent generation because they offer investors flexibility, diversification, and control in their portfolios. Data from the Chicago Board Options Exchange (CBOE) suggests that options investing is increasing at an average of 20 percent per year. CBOE volume typically totals more than 100 million options trades per month.

With options, you can make money when the market is going up, and you can make money when the market is going down. And, boy, can you make a lot of money when you own the right option. If the underlying stock goes up 10 percent, your option might go up 60 to 70 percent.[3]

OK, But What *Exactly* Is an Option?

An option is a contract to buy or sell a specific stock or ETF. Each option controls 100 shares of the underlying stock or ETF. The contract is very specific: it identifies a specific price, called the *strike price* (or simply *strike*), at which the contract may be exercised. It also has an *expiration date* that tells you how long the option is valid. So all options have a set price and a set time period.

Options come in two types, *calls* and *puts*. Calls go up when the underlying stock rises, and puts go up when the underlying stock goes down. If you purchase a call, you have the right to buy 100 shares of the underlying stock at the strike price. Let's use

Google as an example. I buy a call on Google with a strike price at $400 with an expiration date of January 2012. That means that in January of 2012, I can buy 100 shares of Google stock at $400 each. What if Google's real price has risen to $700 a share by that time? I'm loving life because I get to buy it from the guy who originally wrote the contract for $300 less than it is currently worth. A hundred shares multiplied by $300 each (the difference between my strike price of $400 and the current price of $700) equals a gain of $30,000!

Now here's the greatest thing about options. If I had just owned all 100 shares of Google stock from the beginning, it would have cost me $40,000 to purchase them, and they eventually would have gone up in value to be worth $70,000. But with an option I never have to shell out $40,000 to buy the 100 shares. I can buy an option for a low price of something around $500 that allows me to get in on the trade. Options offer an alternative way of investing in common stocks without tying up as much initial capital. If this isn't making sense yet, don't worry: just keep reading and it will become clearer.

For each expiration month there are many different strike prices that you can choose to purchase. For a call option, those strike prices that are below the current value of the stock are called *in-the-money*; those higher than the current value are called *out-of-the-money*; if the value and the option strike price are the same, we say it is *at-the-money*. So to review, a $400 Google strike price would be an *in-the-money* call option if Google's current stock is $425. The investor's position is $25 in-the-money.

Now let's look at the opposite example of a call, which is a put. Puts increase in value when the underlying stock goes *down* in price. If I purchase a put at the $450 strike price and Google's current price is $440, I am $10 in-the-money. The lower Google's stock drops, the more in-the-money my put option becomes.

Since options can be confusing enough, for the rest of this chapter I'm going to give all the examples in terms of option calls, not puts. Just keep in mind that everything is opposite with puts.

So to recap: an option is a contract to buy 100 shares on an underlying stock or ETF at a set price (strike price) on a specific date (expiration date).

How Are Options Priced?

The *premium* is the price that you pay for an option. The premium is paid up front, and it is not refundable, even if you decide never to exercise the 100 shares of the option. The amount of the premium is determined by three factors: intrinsic value, time value, and volatility value.

Intrinsic value is the underlying stock price in relation to the strike price. So if Google's stock is worth $425 a share and your strike price is $400, you have an intrinsic value of $25. *Time value* is the length of time until the option expires. You will pay more premium for more time; if the expiration date isn't for three years, you will pay a much higher amount than you will pay if the option expires in one month. *Volatility value* is how much the underlying stock price typically fluctuates. If Google stock is volatile, then you can expect to pay more for the options, whereas an underlying stock like Microsoft may not be as volatile and therefore its option premium won't cost as much. In sum, we have the following: intrinsic value + time value + volatility value = price of option.

In this example, a Google $400 call option that expires in three months would cost $25 intrinsic value + 3 months' time value + high volatility = 43.00.

The price to add on the option beyond its intrinsic value is decided by the market. There is no scientific way to come up with the price since the view of time value and volatility value is subjective. The final price of 43.00 means that the option would actually cost you $4,300 (43 × 100 shares). A stock that isn't as volatile as Google might have a call option with the exact same $25 intrinsic value and the exact same amount of time remaining, but it costs only 27.00. Option buyers pay up for Google because the odds of its increasing in value are so high. That's why a stock that rarely moves in price has much cheaper option pricing.

The premiums aren't fixed, and they change throughout each trading day. So the premium you pay today will be higher or lower than what you paid yesterday or what you will pay tomorrow. These changing prices reflect the supply of and demand for the option. The point at which buyers and sellers agree is the price for that transaction, and then the pricing process begins again until two more willing buyers and sellers agree. Those who are looking to buy an option enter a *bid price,* and those who are looking to sell an option enter an *ask price.* When the bid and the ask prices line up, the transaction is executed.

The worth of a particular options contract is measured by how likely it is to meet your expectations. That's determined by whether or not the strike price of your option is, or is likely to be, in-the-money or out-of-the-money at expiration. If you end up owning an expired Google call with a strike price of $450, but the stock is only at $425, it means that your option is worthless because you're still $25 out-of-the-money. You might have originally bought the call option three months ago for 43.00, but on expiration day it is worth $0. On expiration day, the option is worth only its intrinsic value.

What Are Option LEAPS?

LEAPS are long-term options: they don't expire for at least six months, and they can be held for up to three years. It is very dangerous to hold an option that is due to expire in fewer than six months because you run a real risk of ending up out-of-the-money with an investment worth precisely zilch. If there is no intrinsic value at the date of expiration, there is no value. So LEAPS investing removes that risk completely by trading only those options that still have at least six months left. Once the option crosses the six-month time horizon, it's time to sell it.

So this is why the example of the option on the 100 shares of the underlying Google stock was only theoretical; it was meant to help you understand what an option fundamentally is. As a LEAPS investor, you will never hold the option to that point of execution where you actually purchase the 100 shares at the given strike price. In fact, I have never exercised my 100 shares. Never. Of the thousands of options that I have invested in, I have never held one of them to maturity.

LEAPS were created by the CBOE in 1990. Unlike traditional options, LEAPS have a lifespan of up to three years and open up a long-term horizon for the option trader without the cost of owning the stock directly. Traders can use LEAPS in multiple ways. They can be used as an outright speculative tool or as a portfolio hedge, and they can be used in various combinations of option strategies. They are a great alternative to options and stocks, combining the best features of each into one easy-to-use product.[4]

The world of options is so complex that many investors are too intimidated to venture into it. You hear about strategies involving covered calls, covered combinations, protective puts, cash secured puts, equity collars, stock repairs, index straddles—it's so overwhelming that many take a quick, pained look and just return to stocks.

But you don't have to master the complexities to get into this game. As long as you understand the basics of how an option is priced, you can track its performance each day just as you would track a stock's performance.

My strategy is to use option LEAPS as a stock replacement. Owning an option is like owning the stock on steroids. Let's say I own a LEAPS option on ExxonMobile with a strike price of $75 and a time horizon of two years. If ExxonMobile's stock was initially below my strike price when I bought the option, it means that my option was out-of-the-money. Let's say ExxonMobil was only at $70 a share, and because there was no intrinsic value, I was able to purchase the option for 0.40, or $40. But then magic happens. ExxonMobil's stock goes up 14 percent, to $80 a share. All of a sudden my option is in-the-money with an intrinsic value of $5. The market price for my option LEAPS is now 5.10, or $510. The value of my little $40 investment just increased 12-fold, and the stock went up only 14 percent! Now, if I had bought 10 of those option LEAPS at 0.40, it would have cost me $400. Once ExxonMobil's stock hits $80 a share, each *one* of my 10 options is worth 5.10, and my total investment is worth $5,100.

Show me another place where you can turn $400 into $5,100 that fast. That's why I refer to options as "stocks on steroids." The performance capabilities are sensational. There is no need to hold them to expiration because you can make all the money you need as the market price of the option fluctuates long in advance of any expiration date.

How Do I Buy LEAPS, and What Are the Symbols?

For most online brokerage sites (E*TRADE, Scottrade, TD AMERITRADE, Schwab, and so on), you type in the stock ticker symbol in the "quotes" box. When it pulls up the stock snapshot, it will show a button labeled "options chains." When you click on the options tab, you will be asked to specify which month of expiration you would like to view along with which strikes you want to view. You can either choose to view all strike prices or only those that are in the safety zone at- or near-the-money. After you select a month that is more than six months away, you will see a listing of all the different LEAPS strike prices, along with their associated purchase price.

Calls are usually listed on the left of the strike price, and puts are usually listed to the right. By clicking on the ask price, you will be taken to the purchase window. Here you must fill in five order inquiries. The first is the order type. If you are buying options, you need to click on "Buy Open"; if you are selling options, you click on "Sell Close." Second, you enter in the number of contracts you would like to purchase. Third, double-check to make sure the symbol is correct. Fourth, enter a limit price type. Don't request to execute a market order for options purchases. Since options are sometimes thinly traded, you will have to wait a while for the order to execute, and you do not want to pay whatever outrageous ask price someone else is trying to affix to an option. Fifth, enter the price that you want to pay in the price box and *then* execute the order.

I recommend entering a price in between the bid and the ask price. Limit prices are usually accepted in increments of 0.05. Options pricing converts into real dollars according to the following scale: 0.50 = $50, 1.00 = $100, 10.00 = $1,000, and so forth.

The symbols for options are generally based on the underlying stock symbols, but they use the letters L, V, W, and Z. It is important to note that due to stock symbol conflicts, there is not always a standard symbol format for LEAPS. A single stock can have different LEAPS symbols depending on what month within the expiration year it expires. This may sound confusing at first, but the CBOE provides an easy-to-use symbol directory that you will get used to.

LEAPS are the same as regular options in that each LEAPS contract represents 100 shares of the underlying stock. The strike prices are set in 2.5-point intervals for strike prices between 5 and 25, 5-point intervals for strike prices between 25 and 200, and 10-point intervals over 200.[5]

When options are listed for trading on a new stock, usually LEAPS are not immediately available. After a period of time, and if interest warrants it, the exchanges listing the shorter-term options may decide to list LEAPS options, after consulting with the market makers or specialists assigned to trade the stock options. The reason for this is that LEAPS options are difficult to price because of their long life. The exchanges ensure that sufficient interest is present in the market, and that market makers or specialists are prepared to price and trade longer-dated options once they are listed.

LEAPS are initially listed with three strike prices: at the current price, and at 20 to 25 percent above and below the price of the underlying stock. Strikes may be added as the underlying stock moves. LEAPS have only one expiration month: January, in two different years.[6]

How Do I Navigate the Investment Climate with LEAPS?

LEAPS are an investment tool that allows you to make money in the good times as well as the bad. In the modern world, where we transmit economic data almost instantaneously, it is vital to have this capability. Renting an option means that the value of the option will fluctuate by a greater percentage than the value of the underlying stock, which gives your portfolio greater price velocity. This gives you power as an investor, but it's important that you wield it with a great deal of care. You should never commit your portfolio to trade LEAPS at the expense of your feeling of security; dedicate no more of your investments to them than your comfort level allows. We all savor the satisfaction of getting the trade right, but you need to keep in mind what can happen if the trade goes wrong. If the underlying stock goes down 10 percent, your call option could lose 60 to 70 percent. The only way you can afford to take the risk of options investing is to make sure your overall investment portfolio is properly allocated between cash, stocks, bonds, mutual funds, and so on. The money you dedicate to options should be above whatever sum you depend on in your daily life.

The ideal moment to invest in LEAPS is when you identify a bargain in the stock market that is too good to pass up. With every LEAPS I own, I'm aware of a particular catalyst that will influence future performance and convinces me that the particular time period will be one of stock price appreciation. The market is a forward-looking entity, and it will price in future catalysts before they even happen. The time in between, during which an investor is waiting for a catalyst to provide its spark, is a great time to own a LEAPS option.

The key is to bet on solid companies that have great prospects for growth during your ownership of the LEAPS option. It doesn't make much sense to own a LEAPS option on a stock that rarely moves because you lose time premium as you approach expiration date. Even if the stock doesn't go down, you can still lose on LEAPS. Most option investors incur losses not because they incorrectly analyzed the direction of the market but because the move they anticipated didn't happen before their option expired. The erosion of time premium is not linear or evenly paced. The erosion in the earlier months of an option's life is much less intense than the erosion that happens in the last few months. This is another reason why we stick with LEAPS.

Time erosion in the last six months of holding an option can be so dramatic that even if the stock rises, the option actually may decrease in value. And this illustrates why options are so difficult for most investors to handle. To be successful, you not only have to be correct about the direction of a stock's movement but you also have to be correct about the timing and magnitude of the movement.

How Do I Calculate the Volatility of LEAPS?

Understanding the concept of volatility in options trading is critical to an investor's success. Volatility indicators provide traders with an estimate of how much movement a stock can be expected to make over a given time frame. This is crucial to determining whether an option is likely to expire in- or out-of-the-money by the expiration date. Understanding volatility also helps traders understand whether an option is cheap or expensive relative to the historical facts of the underlying instrument. *Historical volatility* is a statistical calculation that tells option traders how rapidly price movements have occurred over a given time frame. The most common method of calculating historical volatility is called the *standard deviation.*

Standard deviation measures the dispersion of a set of data points around its average. The more disperse (spread out) the data points are, the higher the deviation. Traders refer to this deviation as *volatility.*

Don't get too caught up in trying to understand the hows and whys of the standard deviation. Just accept that all traders use this method to determine historical volatility. Assets that have large and frequent price movements are said to be volatile, or to be of high volatility. Conversely, assets whose price movements are slow and predictable are said be low volatility instruments.

Why is volatility so important to option traders? It's because it measures the possible price changes of the asset in the future.

Assets that have high volatility can be expected to have large future price changes. As a result, options that are based on assets with high volatility can be expected to have higher prices.

The higher the volatility, the more likely it is that the underlying asset will trade higher (or lower) than the exercise price by the expiry date.[7]

What Are the Different Uses of LEAPS?

Buy Equity LEAPS Puts

You can buy puts to hedge your portfolio against the threat of a down market or to try generating profits in a down market. A hedge gives investors more confidence to remain in the market; it's easier to hold on if you know you have some downside protection. The perfect hedge is an investment that will go in the opposite direction of your long position. For example, if I was long the market but a potential headwind was high oil prices, it would make good sense to buy equity puts on the airlines as a protection for my portfolio. As a rule, I am leery of equity puts. It is very difficult to avoid getting pummeled on the put side by a surprise announcement from the company or any bit of positive news that you failed to anticipate. For this reason, I would rather buy puts on the index that I know will go up in value if the market takes a turn for the worse. Puts on individual companies can be dangerous because you are betting against an entire team of people who are working to succeed. That fact always makes me nervous. For this reason I recommend using equity puts as a hedge and not necessarily as a growth tool. Owning some puts will give you peace of mind.

One of my best catalyst put trades happened back in 2004 when the founder of Martha Stewart Omnimedia—Martha Stewart herself—was convicted of insider trading and sent to prison. I'd kept a close eye on this story since the accusations against Ms. Stewart had surfaced two years earlier. Of course, I wasn't alone; the media was in love with the idea of this upper-class woman, who had built a corporate juggernaut and recently had been named the third most powerful woman in America, might soon be cooking and crafting for fellow convicted felons. Perhaps the most memorable TV clip occurred on June 25, 2002, when Ms. Stewart, being grilled by CBS anchor Jane Clayson, tensely chopped her cabbage and barked out, "I just want to focus on my salad."

At that moment the stock for Martha Stewart Omnimedia was at $13.50. We knew this scandal wasn't going away, so we entered a put position on the stock, as it was now completely focused on its one and only marketable brand. The next day the stock closed down 23 percent, at $10.40. The $10 strike price put options that we had bought were up an astounding 370 percent.

Almost one year later, on June 4, 2003, the government indicted Stewart on nine counts, including securities fraud and obstruction of justice. Stewart stepped down as CEO and chairwoman of her company. Her corporation's stock was still at $10, so we decided to reenter the put position until her trial commenced in January 2004, thinking that the market would continue to price in her departure until it actually happened. By January the stock was $11, so we exited the position at a loss and waited for the uncertain outcome. On the day the jury was to announce its decision, the stock rose to as high as $17 until the guilty verdict was reported; then the stock immediately crashed back to the $10 range.

Stewart entered prison in October 2004, and we knew that the forward-looking stock market would price in her release—she was to serve a five-month sentence—so we bought calls in anticipation of the next six months. From October to March, the stock went from $15 a share to $30.

It's great making an investment that feeds you both coming and going.

Buy Equity LEAPS Calls

You should purchase calls when you anticipate an increase in the price of a stock over the next two years. The option will generate much more of a boost to your portfolio than stock ownership can, and the best thing is that you don't have to allocate as much capital as you would with stock ownership. LEAPS are much safer when they're deep in-the-money because you are assured of owning intrinsic value. I've been known to take some out-of-the-money fliers in my day, but those gambles are extremely rare, and investors must accept that they carry high risk. Using calls should happen when you discover an unusual opportunity in the market. You should understand all aspects of the business opportunity and keep a daily watch of the opportunity's conditions. As long as your initial thesis remains sound, you'll be confident enough to stay invested. As soon as the original thesis is substantially altered, it's time to exit the position.

An excellent example of a LEAPS candidate was Bank of America (BAC) during the first half of 2009. The financial crisis had pushed this once mighty stock all the way down to single digits on the fear that the government would nationalize the bank, and thereby destroy or severely dilute all of the common stock. There was one major problem with this theory. All national leaders, including President Obama, Fed Chairman Ben Bernanke, and Treasury Secretary Tim Geithner, repeatedly stated they were not intent upon nationalization to the extent that the market supposed.

Meanwhile, Bank of America had acquired the nation's largest retail brokerage firm—in Merrill Lynch—as well as the nation's largest mortgage lender—Countrywide Financial—during the crisis. I knew that as we entered into recovery mode, this company was going to be the undisputed leader of the new economy, with earnings potential that far surpassed its capacity before the crisis. Bank of America CEO Ken Lewis had made these acquisitions, although they were unpopular in the short run, because they were long-run game changers. So I bought some January 2011 $5 BAC calls for 0.35 that I plan on holding until midway through 2010. Do the math, and you'll see how much value these puppies will accrue.

Conditions like those of 2009 can make an investment in a long-term option very favorable. In the case of Bank of America, the discount to assessed intrinsic value was very high and made an excellent investment.

Remember: LEAPS investing is a byproduct of an already excellent investment idea.

Buy Index LEAPS Puts

There is no hedge that gives you better downside protection than an S&P 500 Index put. Many investors get into trouble when they try to find the perfect hedge for their long investments. This one rarely fails. This is also a great one to own when the economy transitions from improving to worsening. The volatility created by the downside of such an environment is often pretty nasty, as investors realize that conditions have gone from good to bad.

Buy Index LEAPS Calls

If the market has experienced a broad pullback and all stocks are down, it is best to buy the S&P 500 Index calls for the bounce. This is the easiest trade in the game. During a period of improving economic data, I love to buy S&P 500 calls when the broad market pulls back. Easy money.

Catalysts: React to the Overreaction

Certain, special catalysts can highlight some candidates for options investing in either a growing or a slowing economy. A catalyst can be some sort of legal trouble, product announcement, restructuring, turnaround, sector performance, or other condition that provides an opportunity for alert investors. They create such great opportunities because the market often overreacts in the short run to unresolved challenges. The media and market assume, wrongly, that there are no solutions to many short-term problems and they forget that most problems *do* get resolved because most management teams are capable of making their way out of trouble. Many people, even the very intelligent, focus on problems and worry endlessly about the negative. But if you can look past the short-run inconsistencies and see mitigating factors that affect the long term, you will be able to hit some wonderfully long-run home runs.

Coming out of the recession in 2009, many stocks are undervalued because the broad market pulled them down. You may have to explore unfamiliar corporate territory to find catalysts and the stocks they can spark, but don't look at that as a chore. Searching for catalysts can keep investing quite interesting, and you don't want to limit yourself to one industry or one company all of the time. I think investing in only a select batch of the same companies forever is an overrated strategy. You never know which sector might produce tomorrow's investment grand slam. With the Internet search engines at your disposal, it is relatively easy to become an expert in a previously unknown industry.

At this early phase of recovery, my favorite batch of stocks are those that have been beaten down to single digits, even though their core businesses are stronger than ever. The following stocks represent great LEAPS opportunities over the next two years.

Ford

This was the only large American automaker to elude the brutal grasp of government intervention. Its strong balance sheet helped to avoid bankruptcy and thereby gave it a two-year head start over rivals like General Motors and Chrysler in the recovery. As the other auto companies close thousands of dealerships across the country, Ford will be able to profit from the consolidation. CEO Alan Mulally has done a terrific job of reinventing the Ford brand and dumping off the excess products since he took over the company.

Bank of America

You'll recall from Chapter 1 that when I made my public call to buy Bank of America on February 20, 2009, the day it reached its low of $2.53, many other analysts called my recommendation irresponsible. I paid no heed to their negative commentary and bought the option LEAPS. I wrote that day on TheSteet.com, "What is irresponsible is the fact that so many opinions have jumped at this nationalization threat that is way out in 'left field.' While the masses are running out of the theater, I'm perfectly content to step in and buy my ticket. Obama, Geithner, and Bernanke have all been clear on the underlying principles that they believe can solve this crisis. They are in control of this recovery and I expect they will institute a detailed plan that conforms to the ideals they have verbalized over the last week. If anything, it might be irresponsible to sit on the sidelines and not buy a great bank like Bank of America. Unsubstantiated fear is irresponsible. I am confident that lessons have been learned from Lehman and AIG that won't be repeated. This fear nonsense is so out of whack."

CEO Ken Lewis came out and said he's looking at after-tax profits of $30 billion during normal times for his company! He sees earnings per share (EPS) normalizing up to $5. BAC has $2.4 trillion in assets, with every other American citizen as a client! And today's market cap sits at only $45 billion! All numbers worthy of exclamation marks! That call will be difficult to top.[8]

General Electric

This stock fell to single digits due to a negative balance sheet effect at GE Capital Services Unit. With $680 billion in assets and $51 billion in real estate debt securities, this unit stoked panic in the market, which couldn't handle such a large exposure to the troubled financial industry. It got to the point that investors forgot that GE actually had other working parts in its conglomerate. That's where I came in. GE was down as low as $5.87, even though it's among the world leaders in appliances, energy, health care, and media and entertainment as well as oil and gas. Basically, GE is its own global economy, and this company isn't going anywhere. But when your stock is priced in the single digits, investors start believing that bankruptcy is a possibility. No way on this one. Buy it up.

E*TRADE

A story very similar to General Electric's, but on a smaller scale. Investing in E*TRADE right now is all about one thing and one thing only: bankruptcy. If they avoid it, the stock will at least double over the next year.

I think E*TRADE will survive, and I am buying shares. The core of the company is just too strong. Trading activity in Q1 2009 was up 8 percent year over year with an increase of 63,000 net new brokerage accounts and $3.5 billion in new customer assets. On the mortgage side of the company, special mention delinquencies are down 25 percent since 2008, which should result in reduced charge-offs in the second half of the year. An important part of E*TRADE's strategy is what CEO Donald Layton referred to as a "very active loan modification program that was implemented this quarter. . . . The modifications impacted our financial statements, . . . [giving us] very limited exposure to future write-downs."

My thesis indicates that the future will be brighter than the past for E*TRADE. The hardest part is over; they are still standing after the crisis. Corporate cash is at $406 million, and bank excess risk capital is at $451 million. Without the loan loss provision from the quarter, E*TRADE would have earned $221 million. If they had marked to market in accordance with FAS 159, they would have generated additional income of $500 million. The brand is strong. Their commercials have been a marketing hit, and more importantly, they are driving new customers up to the platform. The fact that they have continued to grow their retail brokerage business in the midst of the financial crisis is to me a clear signal that the core of this company is worth investing in at these distressed levels. Assuming that economic conditions continue to show improvement, it could be an opportune time to put some distressed capital to work in this company, which offers high risk but high reward.[9]

IMAX

Investors should be paying particular attention to IMAX ticket sales. IMAX's relevance to the movie business at large was assured with the release of *Batman: The Dark Knight*. Director Christopher Nolan said, "When you see these sequences on the IMAX screen, it creates a very, very immersive, very much larger-than-life feel for the film. Working with the IMAX cameras was difficult, but we found our feet with it pretty quickly. . . . I actually felt that whatever production issues we would face—which were considerable—they were actually much more controllable in a theatrical fiction film. Even when you shoot in a real location, you put your own light in, you control the whole environment. So I actually think IMAX is pretty well suited to Hollywood filmmaking. And the Hollywood production machine is amazingly efficient, so it was able to absorb the extra demands of IMAX incredibly effectively."

Warner Bros. integrated the 94 IMAX theaters into the advertising campaign for the *The Dark Knight* that spread across television, billboards, newspapers, radio, outdoor, online, and movie theater preshow ads. IMAX has generated returns on Warner Bros.' marketing efforts. Ticket sales went through the roof, and there are hundreds of sold-out IMAX shows across the country with every new release. According to a report in USA TODAY, IMAX has begun a construction boom that will have increased the number of venues in North America nearly 80 percent by the end of 2009 as it installs its proprietary digital projectors in new and existing theaters. That's part of a larger plan to win back the confidence of investors, theater owners, Hollywood studios, and consumers following a period marked by steep losses, a failed attempt at a corporate sale, and questions about the integrity of its financial reports that arose when an SEC inquiry led to restatements.[10]

Consumers typically pay an additional $3 per ticket for an IMAX screening, which means that Hollywood studios likely will make more big releases available to IMAX. They will find it to be an especially appealing vehicle for the growing number of flicks being made in three dimensions. IMAX also is talking to professional sports leagues — executives declined to say which ones — about showing live broadcasts on its supersize screens.

"They're getting great movies," says Merriman Curhan Ford analyst Eric Wold. "The new theater pace will be huge over the next two years. And I predict them turning profitable in the fourth quarter and staying profitable ever after." AMC gave the digital and joint venture package a powerful endorsement with a deal that was unveiled in December 2008. IMAX agreed to deploy its new digital projectors at 100 screens in 33 markets, including New York, Los Angeles, Chicago, Washington, and Miami. In March 2009, Regal, the nation's top theater owner, agreed to joint ventures that call for 31 digital systems in 20 markets. Recent announcements reveal that deals have been signed with Japan and Australia as well.

This company has substantial catalysts for growth. Its current share price, $7.30, represents an attractive entry point. Some of the most influential figures in entertainment are working aggressively with the latest breakthrough in 3D technology, including three-time Academy Award winner James Cameron, U2 front man and visionary Bono, *Lord of the Rings* director Peter Jackson, and IMAX co-CEOs Richard Gelfond and Bradley Wechsler.

For those of you whose 3D experience is confined to watching Captain EO while wearing those paper 3D glasses, I've got news: this new technology will blow your mind. According to U2's 3D executive producer Sandy Climan, "We think this is going to usher in an era of filmmaking that causes a paradigm shift not that much different than silent films to talkies, or black and white to color."

James Cameron agrees: "There will eventually be major titles available from all studios at some screens in almost all multiplex cinemas worldwide. I would say the horizon for this is five years . . . 3D's broad acceptance at theaters will generate enough content that consumer-electronics manufacturers will make home players and monitors available. The technology exists now but is not readily available as off-the-shelf products. 3D display will become a must for video and computer games. The density of information one can place on a small screen becomes much higher if it's stacked in three dimensions."[11]

Choose LEAPS over Margin

Investors always think they need more money. Usually we think that we're in the trade of the year and if only we had a little more throttle, we could *really* make some money. Well, most brokerage accounts are more than willing to lend you the extra cash you need to hit that home run, but I'm here to tell you not to take it. Borrowing money for investment purposes is the ultimate double whammy. Your risk skyrockets when you accept those borrowed funds. If you lose, you lose double because you're going to have to pay back the extra money on top of the loss. This is a classic moment when an investor's stomach can weaken to the point of nausea. Please don't put yourself in that position.

It has become an acceptable practice to invest with borrowed funds on what the brokerage houses call *margin*. They usually allow individual investors to draw on an extra 50 percent credit line to augment investing. If you don't maintain proper levels in your account, they enact emergency margin calls that force you to sell securities in order to pay back your debt.

This is not a sound investment tactic. The time that you allocated to your investment strategy just got cut short. Using margin appeals to greed, but it undercuts good sense. The market is a place known for its wide and fearsome swings, and by now we all should know how fragile the economy can be. Even events overseas can affect us here at home, and quickly. The same volatility that informed my switch from buy and hold to economic timing can rear its ugly head at any time of day or night.

Society has grown accustomed to consumer debt as a normal part of existence, but don't let this complacency spill over into investing. Selective advertising sends out enticing invitations to borrow, but there is seldom any mention of the interest that accrues. For investors, interest payments hang like the sword of Damocles, ready to come down on our heads when we least expect it.

Assuming that only good times lay ahead is foolish. We should plan for the tough times. Nobody knows when emergencies will strike. Nothing brings individual contentment like living within our means. Self-reliance should be your goal as an investor; using margin is not the way to obtain it.

An Executive Summary on Choosing and Buying an Economic LEAPS Option

Assuming that you really are ready to proceed, without further introduction we'll quickly cement the six steps to becoming a LEAPS investor:

1. Identify the direction of the economy in accordance with the principles of economic timing, as outlined in Chapter 2.

2. Research a stock that offers opportunity either because of an overreaction in the marketplace or because of an upcoming catalyst that is consistent with the economic direction of the overall market.

3. After you have chosen your stock, begin to look at the option chains available on most Web sites that offer stock quotes. You'll want to make sure you are not looking at the options that are set to expire within six months because they carry too much time value risk. The ideal LEAPS contract is usually two years out.

4. As you compare different LEAPS, look for good deals on premiums in comparison with strike prices close to your target.

Because the options market is more thinly traded than the stock market, there will be times when one LEAPS contract is better priced than another. For example, let's say I want to purchase an in-the-money Google LEAPS contract that is two years out with a strike price of $400. Because the current underlying stock price is $410 and the time value along with the volatility value are high for Google, the LEAPS option costs 30.00. (10.00 for intrinsic value + 10.00 for time value + 10.00 volatility value. To create numerical stand-ins for time value and volatility value, I simply divide the amount that is left after subtracting intrinsic value by 2. This method isn't precise, but it gets the job done, and it is quick and easy when you are calculating many options.) To determine if I should purchase the $400 strike price, I should compare it with the strike prices directly above and below it. Let's suppose the $390 strike price costs me 38.00 and the $410 strike price costs me 24.00. Which is the better deal? The $390 for 38.00 divides out to be 20.00 intrinsic value + 9.00 time value + 9.00 volatility value. The $410 for 24.00 divides out to be 0.00 intrinsic value + 12.00 time value + 12.00 volatility value. Answer: All three options are equally good values.

Investors should expect marginal increases in the price they pay for time and volatility as they move up the strike price chain. Each incremental move up increases your risk and potential reward. I provided the example above because it is what you will likely encounter in the real world on a LEAPS like Google that is widely traded.

If you were looking for an option LEAPS on a company like Raser Tech that trades on low volume, and you found that the $10 strike price cost 3.00 and the $11 strike price also cost 3.00, which one would you buy? Obviously, the $10 strike price because you are closer to being in-the-money and yet you get to pay the same price as the LEAPS option that is $1 higher. If you are able to identify these kinds of inconsistencies in options pricing, you'll have an advantage.

5. One last thing to consider before choosing your specific LEAPS: volume. When you look up each option chain, you will be able to see the daily volume numbers. If you are purchasing large quantities of options, you better make sure that you are investing in a strike price that other investors also trade. While this isn't a necessity, it is a general rule to keep in mind while choosing your strike price. Even dollar strike prices like $50 usually are more liquid than strike prices like $47.50. You don't want to be caught in a situation in which you are ready to sell out and there are no buyers because of low volume.

6. Now that you know which direction the economy is headed, which company you want to own, and which option LEAPS you want to purchase, it's time to execute the order. Go to your brokerage Web site, pull up the stock quote, click on options chains, enter the month and year of your desired expiration, find the strike price, click on the bid, enter your order type (buy open), enter the number of options you would like to purchase, make sure the symbol is correct, enter limit order, and enter the price you want to pay for the option.

Congratulations! You've made your first foray into the challenging, modern world of LEAPS investing. Here's hoping that it's a remunerative venture.

five

RULES FOR THE PERFECT ECONOMIC LEAPS

N ow that you know how to identify the higher market ground with economic timing and understand how to use the optimal investment tool in option LEAPS, it's time to apply those lessons to the investment strategy I have pioneered: Economic LEAPS.

There are two sets of rules to follow; one set is geared to investing in an improving economy, and the other should be implemented in a worsening economy. Dynamic duos have made a lot of history— Batman and Robin, peanut butter and jelly, Shaq and Kobe, name your favorite—but this duo just might prove to be the most profitable yet. It is: economic timing + option LEAPS = alpha investing.

Nine Rules for Investing in a Growing or Less-Slowing Economy

When economic data shows a rate of change that is improving and stocks are going up based on the positive news flow, the market is in a full-fledged uptrend. Here is the rule set you should apply.

Rule 1: Be Fully Invested

Based on your personal risk tolerance, you can load up the portion of your investment portfolio that is allocated for growth. Think of this as surfing time. There's a saying that's famous in the sport: "Give a man a surfboard and you've distracted him for a day. Teach a man to surf and you can't get him to work." Individual investors who are surfing the right market waves at the right time will want to quit their day jobs. Investing the right way can grow your portfolio by leaps and bounds. (I think this investor-surfer analogy may work on many investors subconsciously and result in a slew of vacation bookings on the beach!) On the new Wall Street, there aren't many opportunities to be fully invested, but this is one. Being fully invested does not mean that you never sell to take profits, nor does it mean that you don't maintain the prudent practice of diversification. But it does mean that it's moneymaking time on the long side.

Rule 2: Initial Cycle Portfolio Position

When you're in the front half of the economic growth cycle, it's time to position the portfolio with these:

Overweight	Underweight
Small caps, midcaps	Large caps
Managed mutual funds	Indexes

Small caps and midcaps get the worst punishment in a downturn, so they typically have more ground to make up in the recovery. You want to own these for the initial pop. The reason you want to own managed mutual funds in the beginning, rather than the index, is because the managers can take advantage of the low-hanging fruit. There are always overreactions in a downturn, and you want to ride those stocks that got unfairly punished on their way back up. As the growth cycle matures, you should shift into large caps that won't be as volatile and ETF indexes because there aren't any fees to pay. Why pay fees to a manager when the low-hanging fruit is all gone?

Rule 3: Latter Cycle Portfolio Position
In the latter half of the economic growth cycle, it's time to position the portfolio with these:

Overweight	Underweight
Large caps	Small/midcaps
Indexes	Managed mutual funds

Rule 4: Seek Leadership
Don't be afraid of high option premiums. Option LEAPS lose a portion of time value every day that you hold them, so it's important to be invested in underlying stocks that will move. Every bull market can be defined by a specific group who leads the charge; make sure you have identified who those fundamental leaders are.

I love the introduction to Alice Schroeder's biography of Warren Buffett, *The Snowball*. It begins, "It is the winter of Warren's ninth year. Outside in the yard, he and his little sister, Bertie, are playing in the snow. Warren is catching snowflakes. One at a time at first. Then he is scooping them up by handfuls. He starts to pack them into a ball. As the snowball grows bigger, he places it on the ground. Slowly it begins to roll. He gives it a push, and it picks up more snow. He pushes the snowball across the lawn, piling on the snow. Soon he reaches the edge of the yard. After a moment of hesitation, he heads off, rolling the snowball through the neighborhood. And from there, Warren continues onward, casting his eye on a whole world full of snow."[1]

Snowball investing is the most profitable method that I know of and is the ideal play for option LEAPS. Own companies that have the potential for an increasing rate of market share growth. Money flows to real growth. If there is no potential for a snowball effect, I wouldn't own the LEAPS.

There is a saying out there that the trend is your friend. It's true, unless you jump on the trend near the end of its life as so many do. The best time to invest is near the beginning of the snowball effect; make sure you're not getting sucked into the euphoria of a bubble. If the fundamental growth prospects don't project well into the future, take caution.

I laughed at those basketball fans in the 1990s who were so infatuated with their home teams that they failed to appreciate the greatness of Michael Jordan. I've never liked the Chicago Bulls, and I probably never will, but I recognized that what I was watching Jordan do out on the court was legendary. When investing, it's always a good idea to follow greatness. Some options investors become obsessed with finding obscure, low volatility options with cheap premiums. I say they're low for a reason and most of them aren't worth your time. There is nothing wrong with investing in an obvious winner. Also, if an initial public offering (IPO) becomes available in the hot sector of the market, you should spend some serious time researching it. This environment of economic growth is a good time to jump on IPOs.

Rule 5: Utilize the S&P 500

A broad market sell-off opens up the door for you to exit some individual LEAPS and buy index LEAPS. This is a tremendously profitable rule during times of a growing or less slowing economy. Let's face it, it is much easier to forecast the broad market than it is to forecast the individual happenings of one company. Owning one company is inherently more risky than owning a batch of 500 companies, which is what you do when you buy a piece of the S&P 500. I employ this rule multiple times throughout the year. Every time there is a multiday sell-off that really pierces investors' hearts, you know it's time to buy some S&P 500 calls.

Rule 6: Double Down by Increasing Your Option LEAPS Risk

When a stock in the common investor's portfolio drops, he usually buys more of that stock in a strategy known as *doubling down*. The wisdom behind such a move is that after an investor's portfolio has been beaten down, he will want to rise up with more propulsion than he dropped with.

With options, you don't necessarily have to add more capital to the position in order to double down. You simply can change your LEAPS call position to a higher strike price. The higher the strike price, the more volatile the percentage moves will be.

Doubling down on a quality stock is a sound strategy, but it can be risky because there's always a chance that the stock will never bounce back. I recommend using this strategy only on high-quality, best-breed companies that have a history of bouncing back. Beware of the one-hit wonder.

Rule 7: Take Profits

Stocks never go up forever. It's important to be disciplined and regularly take gains off the table. Investing 101 tells you to buy low and sell high. Make sure that you are selling high. After all, that is what an up market is for. Your discipline should include a process for averaging into positions and averaging out of positions. Nobody can predict the daily swings of the market, so this will help you build a solid cost basis, and it will help you to systematically take gains.

During an uptrend, I actually take small percentage of gains out of my brokerage account forever. When the going is good, it's time to diversify into alternative investments that can protect your overall wealth. Paps likes to invest in antique cars; I hope to buy up some farmland and produce my own commodities. Whatever floats your boat.

Rule 8: Buy in Anticipation of Catalyst Events

During an uptrend, stock prices will increase in anticipation of an earnings announcement, a product release, or any other catalyst that can produce a type of J.J. Abrams positive uncertainty. These are the mysteries of the market that you want to take advantage of.

The interesting part of investing into positive uncertainty is that the gains are more certain than the gains related to the actual event. In a worsening economy, this rule is the exact opposite. In that climate, you never buy into a long position ahead of a catalyst. You can buy only after all the facts are known.

Rule 9: Watch the Economic Weather

Look out for the direction and rate of change among the various economic data points. To keep yourself in the loop, make sure you check www.economictiming.com. We will keep you updated on the current economic conditions. As soon as the rate of growth begins to slow, it is time to change strategies. Don't get caught off guard.

Eight Rules for Investing in a Dropping or Less-Growing Economy

So now you have an idea of how to function in the boom or soon-to-be-booming times. But as an investor for all seasons, you need to sail through the rough weather as well. When the rate of change of economic data is in decline and stocks are reacting negatively to the news flow, you know that you are in a full-fledged downtrend. Here are the rules:

Rule 1: Cash Is Home

The portion of your investment portfolio that is allocated for stocks should mostly be sold out to cash. In other words, you surfers out there should exit the water and go home until the good waves return. Being fully invested when economic conditions are worsening just does not make much sense. Since it is now becoming normal for down markets to sell off as much as 50 percent, it is a good tactic to remove a large chunk of your portfolio from the market. Go take a long vacation. Go enjoy the cars you bought, or get to work on your farmland. This can be a frustrating time for investors, but there's no use in fighting it; it's one of the cycles we live with.

Rule 2: Protect, Protect, Protect

If you absolutely *must* invest, or "'fly," in bad weather (after all, didn't you get instrument rated for a reason?):

- *Don't go too far from home.* Buy dips and sell rips. Even in down markets there are some short-term sell-offs that provide excellent buying opportunities. Remember that these are short-term trades and not long-term investments. If it doesn't go your way, make sure you have a stop order protecting you from too much downside risk. Also make sure you allocate smaller than average positions to such trades.

- *Invest defensively.* Protect yourself with dividend-paying stocks or best-of-breed companies. In a down market, small-cap stocks get hit especially hard, so it is wise to put your invested money only in the best of the best. Don't fool yourself into believing that these great dividend-paying stocks will be immune from the sell-off; the broad market is quite capable of taking down all ships. In a down market, even good news can get swallowed up in the sea of negativity.

- *Hedge your investments.* You go 100 percent long at your own peril. In a rough climate you should always have some form of protection when you leave home. Identify the downward leadership, and own option LEAPS puts on them. There is always a catalyst influencing economic decline. Identify the key sectors that are affected by this negative catalyst, and make sure your portfolio is positioned accordingly.

Rule 3: Beware of the Falling-Knife Syndrome

Avoid the temptation to call a bottom. Don't trust your heart. Most people are optimistic by nature, but in a down market the only thing optimism will do is trick you into making bad investment decisions. Let the actual data be your guide.

In down times it is difficult to know what prices represent good buying opportunities. Typically a big sell-off will go further than the fundamentals warrant. Investors should exercise extreme caution when they get the urge to buy more stock on the way down because that road might plunge a lot deeper than you ever could have imagined.

Rule 4: Be Leery of High Premiums

Those same option LEAPS that ran with momentum in the uptrend are no longer your friends. Yes, they may be great companies, but they're also used by mutual finds and hedge funds as a liquid way to raise cash when they feel the pressure of investors lining up to redeem their money. In a report published by MarketWatch in the midst of the financial crisis, it was estimated that hundreds of hedge funds would shut down in 2008 as an estimated wave of $700 billion in investor redemptions crashed over the industry. "There's a lot of pressure from high-net-worth and private banking clients redeeming," said Antonio Munoz-Sune, chief executive of EIM Management (USA), a unit of EIM Group that manages $15 billion in funds of hedge funds. "Throw that into the mix and you're seeing good hedge funds facing redemptions of up to 30 percent of assets under management in a market with no liquidity. . . . That's a fatal combination."[2]

It is highly unlikely that your high-premium LEAPS will produce gains in this environment; there are too many headwinds. You will find that the market turns into a sea of negativity in a downtrend. Even the good news gets swallowed up in it.

Rule 5: Stay Prudent with Puts

The temptation in a downtrend is to go fully invested into puts. Well, you should be very careful betting against smart people, which is exactly what you're doing when you own puts.

My growth strategy for profiting from a down economic cycle is not built around using puts. I outperform the market by using smaller than average positions and using puts as a sturdy hedge against further downside. Think for a moment about how many people are working at every single company with the sole purpose of growing the company's business. I'm not wild about betting against that collective brainpower.

Rule 6: All Investments become Slippery

There will be times when the market is so out of whack that nothing works. Puts don't work, calls don't work, and hedges don't work. It all becomes slippery. Sometimes a bear market will be devoid of an identity. A great illustration of this is when President Obama and Treasury Secretary Tim Geithner were initially trying to clean up the financial crisis in the early months of 2009. As I wrote at the time, "They are trying to do a very difficult thing. They are trying to reason with a group of investors who are acting more like a group of drug addicts. Wall Street is obsessed with their next fix. They are never satisfied. Because of this, the markets cannot be trusted in their interpretation of news. The market baited us into believing that we needed to pass an urgent bank rescue plan, and then it baited us into believing that we needed to pass an urgent stimulus plan; the market baits us into believing that once it gets its fix, all will be well. Not true. In the heart of a recession, there are no quick fixes, but that doesn't mean there aren't any long-term solutions.

"So here we stand. Investors trying to understand Washington and Washington trying to understand investors. The current group of 40-year-old, Generation X traders are a mess, and Obama knows it. They are so full of fear from the dot-com fiasco and now this that they have lost all rational ability to manage money. From my experience, the majority of these guys lack conviction, they don't know whom to trust, their greed resembles that of royalty, and their panic attacks have removed all sense of toughness from their makeup. This Generation X group wants to replace anything fundamentally concrete with abstract technical analysis. They are all surface and no depth. It's clear that Wall Street is not at the top of our game, and thank goodness we have a smart guy like Obama who is taking action to fix this thing.

"At this stage of the game it's time for Wall Street to check into rehab and heal from its addiction. The time-honored virtue of patience needs to replace the short-term infatuation with getting the next quick fix. If Tim Geithner needs two more weeks or even two more months to come up with the right banking solution, then he should be given all the time he needs. Don't listen to Wall Street, Tim. They will ditch you and move on the minute you finish your speech.

"Smart investors feel there is a tremendous opportunity to capitalize on the overreactions we currently see. Just because Wall Street has an addiction problem doesn't mean all of corporate

America does. There are segments of corporate America that have never been more fiscally responsible. Compare Apple's Steve Jobs who works for $1 a year with a banking executive like John Thain who was running around like a rat trying to secure his $10 million bonus. Look at Apple's $28 billion in cash. Look at Amazon. Look at Google. Look at IBM. Just because the financials are out of whack doesn't mean the entire country is.

"Investors would be wise to take a step back and gain some perspective on the new Washington–Wall Street dynamic. Washington is attacking all the right problems, and they are working on housing, unemployment, and banking. If they weren't doing these things, we'd be in serious trouble; but they are. Wall Street just happens to be too sick to notice."

Rule 7: Invest in LEAPS with Expiration Dates at Least One Year Out

Any LEAPS you own must have expiration dates at least one year out. Negative uncertainty reigns supreme in a downtrend. Don't pretend that you know when the economic data is going to improve. Make sure you give yourself plenty of time to let it happen.

Rule 8: Watch the Weather!

If you wait until the economic data turns completely positive, you will miss out on the most significant stock moves back up. History shows us that the stock market will recover before the economy does. The market will focus on the rate of change and direction of change to the data rather than the position of the data. Once again, check www.economictiming.com to keep up to date with the latest trends.

• • •

Now you have learned about the economic timing strategy, you have learned how to use option LEAPS, and you have learned the specific rules that guide LEAPS investing in the different economic climates. As an investor, you can't ask for much more than that.

There's an old joke in which a pilot and copilot appear in the rear of the plane and begin walking up to the cockpit through the center aisle. Both appear to be blind; the pilot is using a white cane, bumping into passengers right and left as he stumbles down the aisle. The copilot is using a guide dog. Both have their eyes covered with sunglasses. At first the passengers don't react, thinking that it must be some sort of joke. After a few minutes though, the engines start revving and the airplane begins moving down the runway. Then the plane starts accelerating rapidly, and people begin panicking. Some passengers are praying for deliverance, others are making their last phone call. As the plane gets closer and closer to the end of the runway, the voices are becoming more and more hysterical.

When the plane has less than 20 feet of runway left, there is a sudden change in the pitch of the shouts as everyone screams in unison. At the very last moment the plane lifts off and is airborne. Up in the cockpit, the copilot breathes a sigh of relief and tells the pilot: "You know, one of these days the passengers aren't going to scream, and we aren't going to know when to take off!"

The moral of the story is "no more blind investing." In a world that prides itself on gathering and studying information, I'm amazed that so many individual investors are still blindly committed to buy and hold through downtrending economic cycles.

A New Strategy for the New Wall Street

It's important to remember that we only invest in the stock market for returns. There is no unseen pressure that forces us to invest. This generation of investors has been burned. How badly have we been burned? According to an Asian development bank report, the value of global financial assets including stocks, bonds, and currencies fell by more than $50 trillion in 2008; that's equivalent to a year of world gross domestic product.[3]

According to a study called "The Cost of Active Investing" that was conducted by Kenneth R. French, a finance professor at Dartmouth, investors are being gouged over $100 billion per year trying to beat a buy-and-hold strategy. He took into account the fees and expenses of domestic equity mutual funds, the investment management costs paid by institutions, the fees paid to hedge funds, and the transaction costs paid by all traders. By contrast, in 1980 these expenses came to just $7 billion.[4] To me, this data illustrates the fact that investors know they need to find a better way to invest, and they are willing to spend whatever it takes to do so because the opportunity is so great. The stock market is still a great vehicle to make money, but the traditional strategies aren't holding up.

The four winds of investing—online trading, hedge funds, bubbles, and unintended consequences of government regulation—are responsible for many of the changes in the game. Volatility is the new norm in this era of extremism; to think we're still operating in a twentieth-century economic environment is to kid yourself. In fact, it's more than fitting that the pivotal year of the shift—2000—happened to kick off the new millennium.

Investing over the last 10 years has been torture for those stuck with the old traditions and strategies. But for those who have made a successful shift, it's been a great ride. The only successful strategy is one that is built upon common sense: get out of the market during clear, recognizable economic downtrends, and get in during clear, recognizable economic uptrends. We can't predict daily market moves, but we can recognize the macrocycles of the economy.

The only defensible argument against economic timing hinges on the belief that the sell-offs we have witnessed in this decade won't continue. However, there's no way to prove this, and most people believe the opposite. We are living in a reality where the next downtrend in 2012, or 2014, or whenever it may happen, is likely to cause another market sell-off of 40 percent or more. Volatility has a way of perpetuating itself. Empirical evidence is showing us that this new trend is here to stay. Economic LEAPS is the way to go because this strategy keeps you on the high ground, and it enables you to take advantage of opportunities in a way that is worth your time and energy.

The Investment Advisor of the Future

Once my brother Greg and I were doing some work for our charity of choice, the I Won't Cheat (IWC) Foundation, and we accompanied Dale Murphy, a two-time National League MVP award winner, back to Atlanta for an IWC night at the ballpark. Dale Murphy is royalty in Atlanta; even though he last wore a Braves uniform in 1990, the fans and park staff still love him for his accomplishments and class. Greg and I got to feeling very comfortable, and important, just tagging along with him for the evening.

During some downtime before the game, we were sitting in the dugout looking out at Murph's retired number 3, posted on the outfield wall, and we decided that we'd like to get our picture taken next to it. So we started to walk right across the field. Somehow, we made it all the way to the warning track before a guy from the field maintenance crew sprinted out to stop us. We got more dirty looks on our way back to the dugout than the opposing team got that night. It turns out the royal treatment in Atlanta ends for hangers-on if they dare set foot *on* beautiful Turner Field. That field crew works their tails off every day to make sure each blade of grass is perfect. They treat the infield dirt so delicately that it almost isn't even dirt anymore—I wouldn't hesitate to eat off of that stuff.

Looking back, I really should have known better. I grew up playing Thousand Oaks Little League where a group of parents somehow arranged to get the infield dirt from Angels Stadium imported to our fields. It was amazing to play on the same ground that the big leaguers played on. You can tell when something is properly cared for.

That's how your portfolio should feel: like a perfectly manicured Major League Baseball field. You should be aware of every bit of economic and industry news that threatens to alter your original thesis in some way. I especially love a portfolio after it's been restructured to fit the current conditions; it almost smells like freshly cut grass on a summer day at the ballpark.

You now have a choice. You can adapt your portfolio to the new conditions, or you can hire an investment advisor to do it for you. If you are working with an investment advisor, make sure to get a regular update on the following questions:

- How did your investment performance compare to the major indexes?

- Did any event or economic data point cause you to change strategies throughout the year? If not, why?
- What kind of risk management procedure do you rely upon?
- Do you invest your money alongside your clients'? Are your interests aligned?
- Under what circumstances would you not invest in stocks and why?
- Do you offer option LEAPS investing strategies?
- Do you trade on margin?
- Do you accept cash as an investment class?
- How does your strategy change in a down economy versus an up economy?

Asking these questions will help you make sure you aren't working with an out-of-date investment advisor. Unfortunately, there are too many of these advisors out there. In the old days it was common to meet face to face with your advisor once a year for some small talk and a little update on the portfolio. Beyond the one-on-one meeting, you probably received quarterly performance updates in the mail, and that was about it. Your retirement money was in the hands of an advisor that you barely knew, saw only once a year, and yet trusted completely. It doesn't have to be like that any longer.

Ten years ago Facebook didn't even exist, and Twitter was something only birds did; even the Web was something that still seemed more fitting for a spider than an online investor. Old Wall Street needs to wake up and join the new tech revolution that provides increased transparency and accountability. You can listen to weekly podcasts. You receive e-mail updates. You get links to the important news flow from all the major media outlets as well as from the blogging sites.

Now the biggest problem with the Internet is that it provides more information than most people can digest. This creates another modern function for an investment advisor: to create a relevant context for the information that allows clients to hone in on what is financially meaningful. We all have access to basically the same stuff, but the good advisors are able to see the hidden gems and give the heads-up to clients in a timely manner. Today's Internet-savvy client demands a quick synopsis of the news that has been prescreened by a professional who knows what to look for. The accelerated pace of data transmission and collection has kicked off a new era of individualized service in which you, as a client, should expect to be up to date in every way.

We can now offer better alert systems that improve investment decisions. Do I want to stay in a particular LEAPS after an earnings announcement? What do I think about the latest company plan? What about the increased competition? Questions like these should be discussed openly and actively. As investment management moves online, a much more open relationship is developing between advisor and client.

Speaking of open relationships, I hope that the increased transparency and accountability that comes from online communication can right many of the wrongs we have seen in past frauds perpetrated on investors. I spend a few hours each week working with the aforementioned nonprofit organization I Won't Cheat, which seeks to inject ethics into America's future by educating students on the importance of not cheating in school, in sports, or in life. Through our different activities we educate young people and encourage them to take responsibility for their own actions while reinforcing the belief that their best effort is good enough. It's disheartening to see so many who think that they have to cheat in order to compete. The messages that our children receive from professional athletes who use steroids, from politicians who lie, or from businesspeople who steal are very damaging, not just for the kids but for entire the social structure of our nation.

Adults, meanwhile, have to keep alert in a world where questionable ethics or even no ethics are the rule. It's extremely important for you to keep tabs on the whereabouts of your money. The most frightening reminder of this, of course, is in the form of recently convicted Bernie Madoff, whose Ponzi scheme scandal rocked Wall Street in 2008 and 2009. It was likely the largest investor fraud ever committed by one person. He faces up to $170 billion in restitution for defrauding thousands of investors.

In his plea allocution, which Madoff read to the court, he explained that his scheme began in the early 1990s. He wanted to continue to satisfy the expectations of high returns promised to his clients despite the economic recession. He admitted that he never invested any of the money that he received since the inception of the fraud. Instead, he deposited the money into his business account and paid the clients who requested withdrawals, claiming that the profits were the result of his own unique "split-strike conversion strategy."

Investors could have been spared had they demanded records and updates on the specifics of the strategy. Supposedly, it was a complex one, too complex to unravel or, unfortunately, worry about. Now we know the "strategy" centered on keeping people from searching for a financial strategy that didn't even exist.[5]

There are many heartbreaking stories connected to this tragedy. The story that has most affected me concerns Elie Wiesel—an author, Nobel Peace Prize recipient, and Holocaust survivor. I had the opportunity to meet Wiesel back in the summer of 2006 at a dinner party. When I felt his shaking, frail hand in mine, I was moved to thank him for having the courage to share his story and inspire millions of us to live better lives. It occurred to me that I was shaking the hand of a person who had suffered more than most in world. His most famous work, *Night*, is a haunting look into the evils of the Holocaust and the brutality of the concentration camp where so many his family and friends died. Yet he endured to become what the Nobel Committee called "a messenger to mankind" who conveyed "peace, atonement, and human dignity."[6]

Unfortunately, the evils of humanity revisited Wiesel later in his life (he turned 80 in 2008). He too was an investor with Bernie Madoff. His charitable foundation was another casualty of the Ponzi scheme. In an interview with *Condé Nast Portfolio* in February 2009, Wiesel acknowledged that in addition to having lost his foundations assets, he lost personal wealth to Madoff: "All of a sudden, everything we have done in 40 years—literally my books, my lectures, my university salary, everything—was gone. . . . We gave him everything, we thought he was God, we trusted everything in his hands."

Wiesel said he had met Madoff only twice, and he was introduced to him through a friend who had known Madoff for 50 years and also invested with him. The friend played up Madoff's aura of exclusivity by telling Wiesel, "It's true, you are not rich enough." Madoff gave the impression that he was making an exception by allowing Wiesel to invest with him. Now we know that thousands of others had been lured into this same trap. When Wiesel met Madoff for dinner, the men spoke, ironically, about ethics and education, not finance. During the panel discussion with *Condé Nast*, Wiesel added, "How did it happen? I have seen in my lifetime the problem is when the imagination of the criminal precedes that of the innocent. And Madoff had imagination. . . . We have no idea that a person is capable of that, but then I should have learned, of course, that a human being is capable of anything. . . . I would like him to be in a solitary cell with a screen, and on that screen every day and every night there should be pictures of his victims, one after the other, always saying, 'Look, look what you have done.'"[7]

I hope that we each can learn something from the victimization of Madoff's clients and that the future of investment advisory will include a system of checks and balances to ensure this type of secrecy and fraud cannot be perpetrated. We might be seeing the first signs of that better future now. The mainstream adoption of online trading and the lack of trust are shaking up the financial services sector. And investors have no more excuses for getting suckered into a Bernie Maddoff–like scheme. You now have the capability to review the work of your advisor. You should demand current data and analysis. You definitely should be current about your portfolio's status. Even if you don't want to do it by yourself, you need at the least a basic understanding of what is happening to your hard-earned money. After all, nobody cares about it more than you do. But as you do take more control, make sure you do it the right way.

Many investors have become distrustful of the investment research that comes out of the big institutional firms, and with good reason. It has become all too common for an analyst's report to recommend a position that is traded within the same company. Any report that contains that type of inherent conflict of interest cannot be trusted. In recognition of this, some institutions are cutting back on the quantity of reports produced. As banks cut their research staff, newspapers are going under and old-school reporters are struggling to find profitable distribution channels. All the while, investors are relying more and more on free research distributing on the Internet. Free sites such as Seeking Alpha, MarketWatch, CNBC, and Fox Business are gaining in popularity as individual investors consume and interpret the information on their own.

Whether you're celebrating the new day or mourning for the way things were, the transition will continue on to its unpredictable end. It is more important than ever for investors to have a professional support system to guide them, one that utilizes a method to rate the accuracy and performance of this free research. This is why boutique firms such as Lone Peak are in such high demand. We offer the kind of personalized service that today's client needs, especially to investors who previously relied on newspapers and institutional reports that no longer exist.

It's always a good idea to have a screener give you a second opinion on the market-moving news flow. The big problem with free research is that most media outlets survive based on the number of hits that are generated from each investment article. This makes popularity a greater incentive than substance. A controversial and false article is more important to a Web site than an accurate but boring one. And quite often, successful investing *is* boring. Although the free research flying around the Internet may have made you more knowledgeable than ever before, you must be careful not to overreact to those articles posted for ratings purposes only.

The increasing dominance of mobile high-speed Internet is going to cause a big change in the structure of many industries, ours not least. The Internet takes globalization to the extreme. I can now service numerous clients who live anywhere on the planet because I'm not confined to the limits of travel. No longer do I have to meet with each client in person. We can Web chat once a quarter. We can have a Q&A session through e-mail whenever it's needed. And if we don't speak the same language, we can use the Google translator. Literally, anyone who wants to team with a boutique firm like Lone Peak can have direct access and get to know us on a more personal level than was previously possible unless you lived in the same town and maybe played golf at the same club as your advisor. In the old days, only the biggest firms could engage in extensive outreach. Now, by incorporating the latest technology immediately into our structure, we regional guys can compete with and even outperform the titans. We aren't "regional" anymore, thanks to the technology at our fingertips. In contrast, slow-moving firms governed by inefficient corporate structures are slow getting into sync with the future of investment management.

The Business Is Now Personal Too

Yahoo! CEO Carol Bartz provided a useful insight into personalization when she said, "Yahoo! is the place where millions of people come every day to see what is happening with the people and the things that matter most to them. That could mean what's happening in the world—like breaking news, sports scores, stock quotes, last night's TV highlights—and your world, like your e-mail, photos, groups, fantasy leagues. Based on what we know about you, . . . we can bring you both those worlds. So I think our clear strength is 'relevance'—whether that means knowing what weather to give you or serving up headlines you'll be interested in. It's all about really getting you."[8]

Technology helps Yahoo! and other companies do a better job of tailoring their business model to the individual client. Yahoo! executive Lloyd Braun calls this ability one of Yahoo!'s "secret weapons." In the future, I see investment advisors offering clients a sort of Yahoo! homepage with multiple tools to choose from on a daily basis that have been professionally selected and screened by your advisor in order to ideally meet your unique goals and objectives.

Kevin Kelly of *Wired* magazine writes, "Wikipedia, Flickr, and Twitter aren't just online revolutions in online social media. They're the vanguard of a cultural movement. Forget about state ownership and five-year plans. A global collectivist society is coming—and this time you're going to like it."

There is no doubt that the global community on the Internet has created a new investment culture. The digital world allows cultural and economic trends to spread to the masses in a contagious effect, for good and bad. As investors, we are our own village—a group that shares, cooperates, and collaborates in a collectivist system that is more prone to momentum and fads than ever before. Those who are able to identify the direction and velocity of such economic movements will be in high demand as never before.

Kevin Kelly concludes: "Collaborative social technology . . . is solving problems that the free market couldn't solve. At nearly every turn, the power of sharing, cooperation, collaboration, openness, . . . and transparency has proven to be more practical than we capitalists thought possible. Each time we try, we find that the power of the new socialism is bigger than we imagined."[9]

There is no more faking it. It's time for accountability and performance to rule the investment community. It's time for the real alpha hunters to step up.

six

MONITORING ECONOMIC LEAPS TRADES

Unveil Your Conviction

When the flood of information gets to feel oppressive and the analytical chatter seems unending, I often take a little refreshment by referring back to Warren Buffett and his big-picture, long-term perspective. He doesn't get bogged down in the minutiae of the day, and he always seems to be coming out in the black. We all must find a way to see the forest amidst all those trees in the market.

As an investor, you will sift through data, data, and more data in your effort to formulate investment hypotheses. It's easy to get lost in the many books, articles, and news reports that you take in. There are so many opinions. But you can't get distracted to the point where you've lost your focus on the big picture, and you have to be able to handle criticism if you're vocal about the fact that data and short-term sensations don't tell the whole the story. It seems like any time something extreme has happened in the stock market, Warren Buffett has been criticized for being out of touch. He refused to partake in the dot-com craze of 1999 and 2000 and was blasted in the media. He bought financial stocks in the midst of the financial crisis of 2008 and was blasted again. But who always has had the last laugh? Warren. He could care less about what's going to happen today or tomorrow. He knows that kind of perspective won't ever make you money in the market. The snowballs take time to develop; you can afford to be patient when you're in the right position.

Former President Ronald Reagan was another person who rose above the detail demons. As Californians, many in my family had deep respect for Reagan, who was also the state's governor in the 1960s. So after his death in June 2004, I went out to pay my respects when his hearse passed through the streets of Los Angeles. People were lined up 10 deep to catch a glimpse of the procession, and so my brothers and I took turns hoisting each other up on our shoulders for a better view. The next day my Grandmother Schwarz called to report that my image was in a front-page photo of the *Los Angeles Times*; my 20 seconds up high was good enough to make a little history and pay a small, special tribute to the Gipper.

As president, Reagan took over a nation hamstrung by double-digit inflation. The Reagan Revolution brought economic confidence back to America by reducing business regulation, controlling inflation, reducing government spending, and spurring economic growth through tax cuts. In international matters, he took criticism for describing the Soviet Union as the "evil empire" and inflexibly supporting anti-Communist movements worldwide, but I think history will judge him by his "Tear Down This Wall" address of June 12, 1987. That speech marked the beginning of the end of the Cold War and the decline in the spread of communism; in November 1989, the people did indeed tear down that wall.[1]

Reagan's private journals, which were edited by Douglas Brinkley, provide a fascinating and unique look inside the walls of the Oval Office and into the mind of one of the greatest leaders to serve our country. Keeping a daily log was a productive part of his daily routine. His writings were never complicated. He was a master at breaking down complex issues into simple terms. This skill allowed him to get things done and often to out-think opponents. He lived according to a core set of values that he never deviated from and was disciplined enough to practice them efficiently.[2]

Brinkley writes, "Economical to the core, Reagan filled every page to the very bottom. Reagan was a master of the art of summary. As an orator, he was known to keep notes in shorthand on cards that he kept in his breast pocket. He wrote in the diary in a similar fashion. The very act of composition helped him organize his thoughts as it had since boyhood. He once claimed that the creative act gave him 'great clarity.'"[3]

Interestingly enough, George Washington was also a prolific writer. In the mid-1700s, long before there was a nation to lead, Washington's adventures on the frontier were published as *The Journals of Major George Washington*. His writings thrilled readers in the colonies and in countries as far away as England and Scotland.[4]

Like Reagan, Washington lived in accord with set of "rules of civility," and his regular note taking gave him both discipline and the means to monitor his progress. I don't think it's a coincidence that both of these men were loyal to their core values and they were also both regular writers. A regular examination of one's own life and habits can work a wonderful effect on behavior.

Investors using option LEAPS should keep an investment log to track the housekeeping tasks like expiration dates and premium deterioration. But this is only one part of the investment log you need. You also should document your winning and losing trades, with explanations of why a particular strategy worked or didn't work. I love to go back and read past log entries because, like most people, I'm incapable of remembering the exact circumstances of each day. I also marvel at how often history repeats itself without my being conscious of the fact.

The distortion of memory is a highly interesting and slippery variable that we all deal with in life. By keeping a detailed investment log, we are able to avoid some common pitfalls outlined by Daniel Schacter in his epic book *The Seven Sins of Memory*.

The first sin Schacter outlines, and the most obvious, is the sin of transience. This means forgetting what occurs with the passage of time. Numerous studies confirm what each of us knows to be true: with the passing of time, the particulars fade and the potential for interference increases. Try to remember the investment climate and investment moves you made a year ago. I'll bet you would find a huge difference in what your memory tells you and what you would read if you had kept a journal. Seasonal patterns are of great use to investors because so many forget the past is going to repeat itself. When we forget history, we are doomed to fall into the same traps time and again.

The second pitfall of memory is the sin of suggestibility. "Suggestibility in memory refers to an individual's tendency to incorporate misleading information from external sources—other people, written materials or pictures, even the media—into personal recollections." Inaccurate memories can do a lot of damage to your portfolio. The only thing worse than a bad memory is a false memory. Unfortunately, so much of what we take in from the media is misleading because what's being reported or commented on is the product of *other* people's faulty memory. This can really skew our perspective if we aren't careful.

The emergence of 24-hour financial news coverage on television and on the Internet is nice because it presents a constant flow of news, but what happens when there really isn't any news to report? What happens on a slow day or a slow week or a slow month? You get a lot of fluff that can muddy your thoughts if you allow it in. I'm very distrustful of the financial media and have learned that I must rely on my record of the past to guide me. Those lessons are kept pure when they are written and unaltered.

The third pitfall of memory is similar to the second but contains one crucial extra step; this is the sin of bias. It is committed when "our memories of the past are often rescripted to fit with our present views and needs." Not only are we susceptible to outside influence, but we also fall prey to that influence that reinforces our existing prejudices. This is the sin that investors struggle with the most. In this era of bubbles, most of us have a difficult time recognizing those short-term discrepancies in behavior that JFK was so good at identifying. Here again, a detailed investment log can help. When you review what you did in similar circumstances in the past, you discover that current conditions aren't as abnormal as the pundits would have you believe. Without a record, our current perception will warp the past to align with the present, and the true past will come back to make us suffer.

I am amazed consistently by the short-term focus of market commentators, but I must admit I've come to appreciate the overreactions they foment. After all, they create some great buying opportunities for those of us who can keep the long view in mind.[5]

We don't often have epiphanies, those aha! moments that help determine our future course. (However, we can forget them as easily as anything else, so record them, too!) I've already told you about my big economic timing phone conversation with Paps. Now I'm going to share another that I had at the ripe age of 20. I was attending a conference, and a speaker was discoursing on different methods of obtaining knowledge. He said that we learn by listening, by seeing, and by feeling, and that there is massive room for improvement within the feeling category. The educational system that we all grow up in is biased toward gaining knowledge from listening to lectures or reading words in a book. As most of us grow older, we mistakenly think that this is the primary way to obtain knowledge. We wait around hoping to be enlightened by someone else, and if that someone doesn't show up, we just keep waiting.

In fact, this is a very poor way to obtain knowledge because it is easily forgotten or misinterpreted. Real knowledge is obtained through our own experience. It is taken in through our own senses. The sure way to gain knowledge in your own life is to experience it, feel it, ponder it, and then write it down or teach it to another person.

It's amazing what happens when you extract a general impression from your memory and begin writing it down; details and tangents seem to flow into your mind with ease. Have you ever experienced this? When learning is confined to observation, to what the mind can comprehend in the moment, the returns are shallow and likely ephemeral. When we take the time to contemplate an important event, it takes on new life as it metes out additional insights seemingly without limits. Sometimes in life we need to slow down and take it all in. When we rush through the day, we are living without learning. We become accustomed to glossing over what we hear, see, and feel; soon we've diminished our ability to retain rich memory of even the important events.

At that same conference I first heard someone describe journal writing as a sure way to gain knowledge. But it wasn't until I started keeping one that I began to understand why this is. I discovered the two most important words in our language are *remember* and *organize*. Failure to remember lessons of the past puts you in danger of making large-scale mistakes. Failure to organize inhibits productivity. Journal writing ensures improvement in both remembering and organizing. I never would have come to that realization had I not written down my general first impression that I should begin writing a journal. The ability of the human mind to build upon foundational thoughts is a remarkable tool that we all have at our disposal if we know enough to use it.

So from one piece of advice that I received when I was 20, a way of life blossomed. As I look back, I see that most of my decisions have been influenced in a positive way by some seminal piece of information that I stopped to record and think about. The events of our life can be captured, at least in their essence, if we put them to paper. If we then decide to study what we've written and expand upon it, a wealth of learning material can be captured. When we spend more time reading other people's thoughts and remain unaware of our own story, we lose out.

Doing anything one time is never enough to be worthwhile. The Oxford scholar C.S. Lewis, author of *The Chronicles of Narnia*, said, "I can't imagine a man really enjoying a book and reading it only once." By the same philosophical token, I can't imagine a person enjoying life and thinking about his or her experiences only once. Our experiences deserve to be digested intellectually, our thoughts deserve the attention of subsequent thoughts; when this process is approached with seriousness and discipline, real personal insight and knowledge will flow.

The ability to turn our thoughts into strategic action is crucial to investment success. Thoughts are at the root of all action. Clear thinking leads to clear action. Hedge fund manager Mark Sellers gave a particularly apt description of this phenomenon in an address at Harvard Business School:

> [It's] important to have both sides of your brain working, not just the left side (the side that is good at math and organization). In business school, I met a lot of people who were incredibly smart. But those who were majoring in finance couldn't write worth a damn and had a hard time coming up with inventive ways to look at a problem. I was a little shocked at this. I later learned that some really smart people have only one side of their brains working, and that is enough to do very well in the world but not enough to be an entrepreneurial investor who thinks differently from the masses. On the other hand, if the right side of your brain is dominant, you probably loathe math, and therefore you don't often find these people in the world of finance to begin with. So finance people tend to be very left-brain oriented, and I think that is a problem. I believe a great investor needs to have both sides turned on. As an investor, you need to perform calculations and have a logical investment thesis. This is your left brain working. But you also need to be able to do things such as judging a management team from subtle cues they give off. You need to be able to step back and take a big picture view of certain situations rather than analyzing them

to death. You need to have a sense of humor and humility and common sense. And most important, I believe you need to be a good writer. Look at Buffett; he is one of the best writers ever in the business world. It's not a coincidence that he's also one of the best investors of all time. If you can't write clearly, it is my opinion that you don't think very clearly. And if you don't think clearly, you're in trouble. There are a lot of people who have genius IQs who can't think clearly, though they can figure out bond or option pricing in their heads.[6]

An unfortunate by-product of a world that has become increasingly tolerant is that many people have lost their ability to make a decent judgment call. The rhetoric of political correctness eschews being judgmental; I tell you the opposite. When we avoid the simple fact that life is all about making judgments, we are only hurting ourselves. Exercising our ability to choose is what makes life worth living. I'm going to try to awaken the hard-core decision maker that's slumbering inside and show you how writing can bring it back into the action.

Not surprisingly, a world that shies further and further away from any hard-line judgments visits a great deal of volatility on the stock market. Let's consider a few generational trends. According to an item in *US News & World Report* released in May 2009, the fastest-growing religion in America is no religion at all. The American Religious Identification Survey claims that "no religion" jumped from 8.2 percent in 1990 to 14.2 percent in 2001, and it has now reached 15 percent. "Many people thought our 2001 finding was an anomaly," Ariela Keysar said. "We now know it wasn't. The 'Nones' are the only group to have grown in every state of the Union."[7]

To my thinking, religious statistics are a telling measure because religion is one thing that can force people to deal responsibly with consequences of their actions. Those who don't like responsibility don't like the rules of religion. They would rather live without the scrutiny of accountability. According to another study by the Pew Research Center released in June 2009, Americans of different ages are increasingly at odds over a range of social and technological issues. Religion is a far bigger part of the lives of older adults. About two-thirds of people 65 and older said religion is very important to them, compared with just over half of those 30 to 49 and 44 percent of people 18 to 29. "Around the notion of morality and work ethic, the differences in point of view are pretty much felt across the board," said Paul Taylor, director of the Pew Social and Demographic Trends Project. If you don't make any judgment calls in your personal life, then you won't make any judgment calls of consequence in business either.

Instead of tackling judgments that really make a difference in our lives, too often we try to stay somewhere near the safe middle ground by focusing on judgments of least importance. If you are losing precious hours to the mind-numbing appeal of celebrity gossip, video games, random Internet surfing, or even too many fruitless tasks at the office, you probably need an adjustment. All of these things can suck your mind dry. There are bad uses of time, there are good uses of time, there are better uses of time, and there are best uses of time. Concentrating on actions and events that have consequence is among the best uses. The goal of a great investor is to use his or her time wisely by identifying, analyzing, and confronting real issues. Alpha investors need to develop confidence in their decision-making abilities.

The word *alpha* is not one I employ lightly. Achieving alpha is not like the cursory or false successes that are most often our lot in life. Achieving alpha signifies real understanding. It is a victory over irrational volatility. It demonstrates a calm in the midst of the storm.

Do you recall those motivational posters that were really popular in the 1990s? One of them had a picture of a climber above the words "Perseverance: What the mind can conceive and believe, it can achieve." Another, picturing a beach, declared, "Destiny: Destiny is not a matter of chance; it is a matter of choice." One day my wife and I were out shopping for furniture, and we ran smack into a supersized, eight-foot by three-foot version of another one that pictured a narrow spit of land with high cliff sides. The land was being buffeted by enormous waves that crashed so high that the water seemed to cover all but the tops of the cliffs. This was an image that really displayed the power of the ocean. But most arresting was the presence of a lighthouse near the ledge, surrounded by a plot of perfectly manicured grass. I looked at the picture and knew that it had to hang in my office. That narrow outlet of land seemed to rise above the chaos and stand alone in peace.

An escape from the frenzied, chaotic stock market culture is exactly what all alpha hunters hope to achieve. A key to the journey is the creation of an investment log. It will become your lighthouse in the midst of the crashing waves.

The Voice in Your Head You Want to Hear

If you met Pinocchio in the novel or the film when you were growing up, you probably remember that nose of his. But what I remember best is that faithful Jiminy Cricket is instructed by the Blue Fairy to teach Pinocchio what a conscience is. A conscience in Pinocchio would complete his transformation from puppet to boy because a conscience would make him become brave, true, and unselfish. Naturally, poor Jiminy is forever being frustrated when Pinocchio finds trouble time and again because he refuses to listen to his small, but wise advisor.[8]

I wonder if our consciences feel the same way about us. I think it's safe to say that all of us would be better off if we heeded the guidance that comes to us from our conscience, but of course that's not how we usually act. Sometimes it's been so long since we tried to listen that we forget it's even there, but I promise you that it is. It's a gift worth relying upon, and it's yet another that we can receive by committing ourselves to writing down our thoughts.

Here are some of the best reasons to keep up your log:

- To gain a clear vision of reality
- To help you become accountable and disciplined
- To derive knowledge from what we see, hear, and feel
- To improve your ability to make judgment calls
- To avoid the pitfalls of memory
- To unlock the guidance of our conscience

Writing is a link between clear thoughts and decisive action. I'm not saying this is the only way to do it, but it is the best procedure I can find.

How to Create Your Investment Log

The log is meant to capitalize on the power of thought by harnessing memory and organization. I recommend you develop distinct, individual sections, as follows.

Section 1: Sort through the Clutter

Record the worthwhile ideas that you find while reading or thinking about investments. Don't believe that your conscience is its own independent entity. If this were the case, then everybody would live according to his or her own moral standards. But we don't. The collective, universal conscience seems to agree that murder is bad, stealing is bad, service is good, peace is good, and so on. Because of reality's collective nature, I think of conscience as a radio rather than a contained, isolated source. A radio is a transmitter that can tune in to broadcast stations when it is set to the corresponding frequency. If the radio is set to a frequency with no broadcast, all you will hear is static. Investors need to refine their ability to tune in to the right channels.

You need to keep churning out and through investment thoughts until you find the right broadcast. The access to investment news is now almost unlimited with the Internet. On any given day, I will read over 300 investment news articles, and as I do so, I will sort through the clutter to find investment strategies that resonate with my common sense. I'm trying to search through all the static to find a station that I like. This effort does not yield success overnight. It can take a lot of practice to learn how to separate the legitimate judgments from the fluff.

What defines a legitimate judgment? For one, it will relate to a company with prospects for real growth. Good judgments will take clear shape the more you study them and the more you analyze the thesis. If you have a good idea on hand, your conviction will become stronger with time. If you have a good business, it will produce. This is what defines good judgment. Bad judgment is antigrowth. It's actually not that difficult to discern. Any thesis that is based on proven fundamentals such as increasing growth rate, value, and productive product mix is worth looking at.

So section 1 of the investment log should be a collection of good ideas from your daily reading. You should keep track of important news from companies that you already own, and you should also be looking for companies that you'd like to own. In conjunction with the linked news item, this section should incorporate a single line that states your initial investment thesis. Joe Trustey, managing partner of the private equity and venture capital firm Summit Partners, describes this section's use in one short sentence: "It tells me why I would want to own this business (or stock)."

I agree with Jim Cramer when he says there is always a bull market somewhere. There is always a way to make money in the stock market, but we need to be looking in the right place. It may be counterintuitive, but the Internet doesn't always help us to find that right place because there are no screens on the information it provides; it floods us with more information than we need. A well-oiled conscience is needed more than ever to help us sort through the never-ending flow of data.

You can never predict when the good judgments will strike you, and that's why your investment log needs to be mobile. Lately I've been using the notes section on my iPhone to record my most valuable thoughts. I was coaching my son's soccer game when I thought about buying Apple; I was out to dinner when I thought about shorting oil; and I was at Home Depot when my mind grasped the significance of mark-to-market accounting for bank stocks. We do not get to choose the timing of ideas, so we must be ready for them at all times.

Writing down our important thoughts not only helps us to remember them but also often prompts subsequent thoughts. Keeping a record is a skill to be learned, and with practice you can become perfect. Even the most capacious minds are limited in what they can retain and for how long, but when we respect and value our thoughts, our mental capacity expands.

Many of you have probably applied the discipline of writing out your thoughts to other pursuits. If you want to be better at playing golf, pay attention to the rounds you play and the useful advice you hear. If you're determined to be a better parent, you should record some of the interactions you have with your kids and listen to what your conscience has to say. If you've already grown a successful business, likely there's a record of development plans and innovations you had along the way. Personal inspiration is a tremendous tool that must be consciously applied; don't let it go to waste by failing to record your initial thoughts.

After reading through 300 articles, it would be easy for me to forget even the best ideas I find and thereby forfeit the gains of initial conscience judgment. What a waste of my time and labor. To be productive, you need to write it down and review it; soon you won't let a gem pass you by.

Section 2: Expand Each Thesis to Include
Questions and Personal Impressions

After you have narrowed down the news flow to a few clear, concise thoughts, you need to craft an equation to contain them. In other words, it's time to make the investment strategy your own. It is in this section that we seek to link the flow of ideas coming from our own conscience to the research we've undertaken. During this process, the initial idea or strategy either expands and becomes more enticing or implodes on the paper in front of you.

The ability to exercise restraint divides the great investors from the mediocre. My favorite illustration of this point doesn't concern an investor but rather Apple CEO Steve Jobs, who is famous for his ability to identify the next big trend in technology. He has a stable of brilliant minds working for him at Apple, yet he is very slow to adopt their innovations because he's interested in only those products that will end up being industry game changers. Anything less will not work for Apple. A mediocre product would hurt the brand and blight the ever-expanding growth of his company. Jobs has a supreme gift for restraint.

The collective conscience is always speaking; if we aren't born with an ability to channel it, we must learn. Steve Jobs is able to figure out what consumers want before they do themselves. How could any human ever know such a thing? Nobody ever tells you what the next big thing is. You can't read it in a book. You have to catch the inspiration and then figure out the details in your own mind. Section 2 is something like a lab where you shine a bright light on your find and try to determine if it augments your existing knowledge.

Section 3: Go Back to the Internet for More Company Research

Once you are confident that you have a thesis that you think will work, it is time to start performing in-depth research. Section 3 is the process of going back to the Internet to look up additional sources that can further expand what you already know about a particular company. You'll find some who agree with you and some who disagree with you. Make sure you can reconcile all arguments for and against your thesis before deciding to buy option LEAPS. Does this new opinion change the foundational premise that your strategy is built upon? If it does, then it's time to rethink your investment.

A good idea will turn into a good game plan after it has passed through the rigors of analysis. A bad idea won't survive the process. We all have our favorite investment research sites, but when I'm active in research, I like to veer away from my favorites and try to find any and all commentary about my company. This is when search capabilities are tremendously useful. After this process is complete, you should have written down your initial one-line investment thesis followed by your own impressions of the stock and a compilation of research performed by others. If your initial one-line thesis for owning the company is still valid after these steps, you have a serious candidate for your portfolio.

Section 4: Make Note of the Market-Moving News of the Day

Section 4 is my macroeconomic section. In it, I write down the question of the day and the simple market-moving issues of the day. I like to have a list of about three to five that I believe are the market-moving news stories of the day. (This section of the log is divided by date, whereas the previous three log categories are divided by company.) It is also in this section where I keep track of my 10 economic indicators with a rate-of-change arrow affixed. Keeping an archive of these economic indicators gives me a quick and easy way to know the economic weather.

I like to end my log session with a review of the macroeconomy because I know that no individual stock can overcome the power of the macroconditions. If macroconditions have changed, I better be the first one to know about it.

Section 5: Record the Action

Now it's time to take action and purchase the LEAPS. This is where all of your time and effort come to fruition. By this point, you should be able to argue your thesis front to back. You should feel confident that you are correct and everyone else is wrong. In fact, the best investments happen when everyone else thinks you're crazy; if you've carefully taken the preceding steps, you'll know you're the first to jump on a new cycle.

Once I enter a position, I keep track of the expiration dates with my own personal price targets for each. This helps me to remember what my expectations were when I originally entered the position. Remember the sin of bias? Your current perceptions will kill you when it's time to sell a LEAPS contract and take gains. Current perceptions usually lead you to believe that the stock can go up forever. They never do. This is why it's wise to always check back with your log and remember your original expectations. In my experience, my original expectations are a remarkably accurate indicator of what price I should sell at.

On a weekly basis I will break down the option LEAPS premium into intrinsic value, time value, and volatility value. This is especially important when tracking time value. If I see that I'm losing more than I'm comfortable with, I know it's time to sell out of these LEAPS and buy some that give me a longer time horizon.

These five sections of the investment log aren't rocket science, but they accomplish the objective. Your own version of this template should supply you with the necessary information to make good decisions.

Surprise: The World May Be Waiting for You

In my early days as an investor, I was more of a reader than a writer. I had always known that I wanted to write because I knew that doing so would help me think and act more clearly. The famous quote by Socrates "The unexamined life is not worth living" always stuck with me. My problem was that I wasn't a good writer: another gift never given! Going through school, I never impressed a professor with my innate ability to write, and my grammar is subpar at best. So when I began writing in a journal, I had no intention of writing a single word for public consumption. Then I found Seekingalpha.com. The quantity of the articles the site posted provided me with a terrific brainstorming tool. Brainstorming is my alpha and omega reason for watching and reading financial media. I don't expect anybody to do the work for me, but I do like to delve into groupthink and evaluate the best and worst of what I've seen and heard. After enjoying the content on the site for quite some time, I decided to start my own blog as a way to further enhance my investment log.

I believe the popularity of blogs exploded in no small part because most people were sick and tired of having their news force-fed to them. When I watch the nightly news, I have a hard time relating to any of the stories. All of the unfortunate accidents and murders are sad, but I don't really want to be depressed when I sit down to catch up on the news of the day. Local news outlets seem to do a particularly terrible job of collecting the real news of the day. They place so much emphasis on the lurid, negative stories that there's barely any airtime left for the 100 positive stories that are breaking. So now, bless them, blogs and Facebook and Twitter allow us to pick and choose our news.

I sat down in front of the TV one night with my wife, after I had written my first few blog entries. We were watching *American Idol*, and I was amazed at how the show was pushing Apple's products. Ryan Seacrest was holding up the new iPhone, all of the songs could be downloaded off of iTunes, and Apple's logo was constantly superimposed onto the screen. I wondered if anyone had written about Apple's latest marketing scheme, so I searched the Internet and couldn't find anything. Then I thought, maybe I'll try and write up an article and submit it to Seeking Alpha. Here is a draft of the first article I ever wrote:

Apple Strikes Advertising Gold

As the marginal effectiveness of television commercials continues to decline due to the adoption of DVR, it is more important than ever to be creative in methods of advertising. Look no further than the king of innovation, Apple's CEO Steve Jobs, for the latest example of one who understands this evolution.

On February 18, the partnership between Apple and *American Idol* was announced somewhat under the radar. *American Idol*'s Simon Fuller and Steve Jobs came up with an agreement that gives iTunes exclusive rights to sell *Idol* performances online along with Apple product placement and promotion during the show. With this week's airing of "Idol Gives Back," Apple is embarking on the sweet spot of this deal as the finale gets closer with only eight contestants remaining. Last year, "Idol Gives Back" raised $76 million for charity as ratings soared.

This year's episode will be even bigger and more ambitious as Robin Williams, Celine Dion, Forest Whitaker, Billy Crystal, Dane Cook, Kiefer Sutherland, Vanessa Hudgens, Ashley Tisdale, Jennifer Connolly, Elliott Yamin, Fantasia, and Amy Adams join previously announced international talent and sports figures Bono, Brad Pitt, Reese Witherspoon, Miley Cyrus, Mariah Carey, Eli Manning, Peyton Manning, Fergie, Chris Daughtry, Carrie Underwood, Annie Lennox, John Legend, Snoop Dogg, Maroon 5, Heart, and Gloria Estefan.

During this economic downturn, it is important to remember that Apple is a market share play. Even if weak consumer spending erodes overall demand for computers and phones, Apple could still flourish in such an environment as they march up the ladder of share gains. The *American Idol* partnership further cements Apple as the "king of cool" and will only help the aforementioned cause.

In his predictions for 2008, the founder and president of Seabreeze Capital, Doug Kass, mentioned: "With the economy weakening and corporate profits tumbling, investors pay up—real up—for growth. . . . Apple Computer will move into bubble status, . . . [its] shares doubling in 2008 even as most equities decline."

Earnings season is now upon us, and I expect many companies to report weak first quarter results based on the timid consumer and high commodity costs. This broad market theme should create a final entry point for those who want to be long Apple for the rest of 2008. I will be aggressively adding to my Apple position during any April weakness; I see this stock climbing to $300 by January 2009. There are too many catalysts to ignore. I will provide more in-depth analysis in future articles.

Source: Seeking Alpha Web site, April 9, 2008.

Much to my surprise, Seeking Alpha published it the next day! It was so cool to see my own words published, and I was shocked when the article started to fly across the Internet. Because I mentioned all of the celebrity names, my article was linked on each of their personal Web sites. My wife and I had a good laugh over that one. I was on Eli Manning's Web site right after he had just won the Super Bowl. I was on Carrie Underwood's site! Hilarious but true.

After getting lucky on my first try, I had to find out if it was a fluke, so I tried another one. Sure enough, it got published as well. Eventually my stuff started reaching some mainstream sites; on one of those early days, I had the lead article on Google News for the entire market. I was building a following of readers, but most important, I was more in tune with my investment strategies than ever before. My research had to become that much better in order to defend my calls against opposing voices.

I encourage all investors to start up a blog and write out their ideas. In this day and age, you never know who's reading, and you never know where your ideas will take you next.

seven

BUBBLE INVESTING

Time Traps

The intrigue of turning back time has curiously bedeviled humanity for eons. Time travel has been a conceptual foundation for much of science fiction, going back to H.G. Wells's *The Time Machine*. (Why, even Charles Dickens sent Scrooge on an impromptu journey with the Ghost of Christmas Past.) Modern audiences came out for the thrills of the *Back to the Future* trilogy; if you saw the second installment, I'm sure you drooled while thinking about what you'd do with the *Grays Sports Almanac* that Biff got his hands on. It's too bad that hard science doesn't seem to allow for the experience in real life. Einstein's theory of special relativity infers that one-way travel into the future is possible because of time dilation and velocity in space, but backward trajectory doesn't seem to be allowed. Not in the physical sense, anyway. In the mental sense, however, going back in time happens every day. For me, as it is for pretty much everyone else in the world, the past is a much-visited destination that can sometimes feel like the well-known verse from Proverbs 26:11, "As a dog returneth to his vomit, so a fool returneth to his folly."

Our forecast for 2008 was spot on; I should have known better. We were planning on a year with contracting growth along with the continued disintegration of the real estate bubble, so we had positioned our portfolios for a worsening economic backdrop. We held out hope for a few percentage points of index growth, but we saw that some negative market returns were more realistic. Everything we managed was aligned to withstand the likely downtrend in the economy except my own personal portfolio. I thought I could make some huge gains in January and then close up shop for the rest of the year. I wasn't willing to adjust my equity position to low-risk allocations just yet.

Faced with declining economic data, the market immediately began to tank as soon as it opened for business in the New Year. Even though the economic readings were still in positive territory, the market acted as if everything was about to fall off a cliff when it opened for business on January 2, 2008. The market interpreted good news as bad, and bad news as worse. As investors were busy pricing in the future weakness, I was blinded by greed in the present and could not figure out why the market was acting so irrationally. For the next 450 days the market went into its worst downward spiral since the Great Depression.

I went heavy into Apple during January mainly because of the catalysts. I had loaded up for what I hoped would be 15 more days of rally. Then I would get out. Paps got a ticket to the big Macworld conference in San Francisco that year while I stayed back at the office and steered the ship. Over the years January had been very,

very, *very* good to Apple stock; usually it had soared on the anticipation of the fourth quarter earnings report and on the new product
releases at Macworld. We assumed that 2008 would give us more
of the same. In a window like that, the stock typically rises around
20 percent, and the option LEAPS can double and triple their
values. January 2008 looked to be especially big because it was the
first holiday season for iPhone sales, and we also anticipated huge
Mac sales from the holiday shopping. We expected the unveiling of
the ultrathin business laptop that promised to bump the MacBook
line up to new levels of market share. Yet again, Apple CEO Steve
Jobs didn't disappoint. He showed off the new MacBook Air that
was so thin it could fit in an envelope. Paps called me after the
show and gushed about how it was the best presentation he had
ever seen and how this was the best company on planet Earth and
how they were going to take over the world, and on and on.

I was also gushing, but not the same way as Paps. I was gushing
blood as the stock sold off in a way that was uncharacteristic
of Apple. It was getting swept up into the sea of negativity that
had overcome the rest of the market. Oh well, we decided. We
figured to make up these losses at the end of the month during
the January 28 earnings release and then get the heck out of
this market.

I bought even more Apple before the earnings report because
I was really anxious to compress solid 2008 gains into that one,
single month. I owned some out-of-the money option calls that
weren't even LEAPS. They were set to expire the very next month,
and I was holding on to them because I wanted to go out not just
with a bang but a towering grand slam. Instead of respecting the
forces that were creating a truly negative climate, I put my blinders

up and tried to fight back against the economic conditions with the one company I thought could buck the trend. Of course, January ended up nailing us with two doses of extreme sell-offs. I ended up losing big money because I was so hot to clean up even when all the indicators were against me. Greed overpowered obedience and common sense—an all-too-common failing in this world.

There's one way I use the phrase "going back in time" as a pejorative: it's when you abandon what you know to be true and backslide into an earlier, immature way of thinking and mess up the present. I went back in time in January 2008, and I should have known better. It's essential to understand and accept this concept if you want to thrive in today's stock market, especially when we're talking about bubble investing. The trick is to realize that bubbles frequently mask the fundamentals in the short run but that those fundamentals always rule the long run. Bubbles seem to be creating a new trend for investors to deal with, and they must remember that sooner or later they burst and normal activity resumes. You simply cannot afford to gloss over the lessons that our bubble era has to teach us unless you're willing to suffer by "going back in time" yourself.

Growing up I had a strange talent. I could remember the number of any sports player I had ever seen. Family and friends would throw out the names of obscure bench players to try stumping me, someone like Ron Grandison of the Celtics (number 31) or Mychal Thompson of the Lakers (number 43). Just recently my brother-in-law, Darren, made a bet that I couldn't remember the numbers of the Chicago Cubs' starting lineup in the late 1980s. This wasn't a bunch of superstars, and most of the players have been out of baseball for 20 years, but unfortunately for Darren I didn't even break a sweat. Even when I couldn't remember the face of a particular guy, his number would flash right into my mind.

That mind trick was a lot of fun when I was a kid, and as I've grown older, it hasn't faded. I can still remember all of the numbers of all of the teammates I ever had while growing up, I can remember all of the numbers of the kids who played on the opposing teams and on my brothers' teams. I live with a small ocean of numbers to keep me company. I don't try to keep the information fresh; it's just there, instantly retrievable whether I want it or not.

The scientific name of this involuntary physical experience is *synesthesia*. It's been the subject of numerous studies that have been conducted to find out what it can tell us about consciousness, the nature of reality, and the relationships between reason and emotion. Synesthesia melds the senses into a unit in which one sense causes an additional perception in a different sense. For example, a person with synesthesia might describe the color, shape, and flavor of someone's voice.[1]

I think it's worth discussing some ways that this phenomenon might illuminate investor psychology in the midst of a bubble. Let's introduce Mark Sellers's list of great investor traits. The first trait is the ability to buy stocks while others are panicking and sell stocks when others are euphoric. The second is having an inherent sense of risk based on common sense, and the third, which is the most rare of all, is the ability to live through volatility without altering the investment thought process.[2]

Synesthesia is an unusually vibrant linking of past experience with the present. Investors need to simulate that link to be able to stand fast during the short-term divergences in the stock market. Recall the four winds of investing that we discussed in Chapter 2:

the third wind establishes that we all must deal with the speculative bubbles that take over the market. During a bubble, the market can get its pricing very wrong in the short run, but a commonsense recollection of the historical fundamentals will allow you to profit from such overreactions.

The Oil Bubble of 2008

This principle is what allowed me to identify and profit from the oil bubble of 2008. The high price of crude oil was on everyone's mind, and I was having the most difficult time reconciling this price action with history. There were no lines at gas stations as there had been in the 1970s, oil companies had booked drilling equipment out through 2012, and I counted eight major oil finds within the previous two years. Alternative energy technology was coming on strong, and we all knew that there were certain gasoline price levels that would cause consumers to drastically limit their mileage. In short, this was a classic bubble. The price action in crude oil had become the investment of choice for those seeking momentum. Well, this was some momentum all right, but it deviated from historic norms.

Fifty-three new commodity ETFs were trading as billions of new dollars in demand flowed into them. The oil spike was really hurting the global economy as other commodities such as food and metals had begun to inflate. It's important to note that in this instance too, the media and analyst communities seemed to believe that the trend would last forever. They focused so avidly on the rationale of the speculators driving up the price that they ceased to view the trend in a historical context.

The following are excerpts of my writings from that time. They'll provide some useful descriptions of the reasoning and research that are required to formulate a surefire investment thesis that employs the function of synethesia.

Should We Listen to Boone Pickens on Oil?

I love T. Boone Pickens. He has had a remarkable career, his philanthropic efforts are far-reaching, and the Pickens Plan offers a great future for our country. There's just one problem with his repeated claim that oil won't ever go below $100 a barrel: He has a severe conflict of interest. Those who are banking on this man's crude oil forecasts are at risk because of it. Like clockwork, Mr. Pickens appears on CNBC when oil has a big down day to tell everyone that oil will be headed back up. On Tuesday his rationale was that it's fun for OPEC to make billions and billions of dollars. He predicts they will cut production to maintain the high price.

Anyone who has followed the oil spike knows that OPEC lost pricing control a long time ago. As they increased production, oil prices still continued upward. So why is Mr. Pickens telling us that oil will stay above $100? Because the Pickens Plan has everything to gain from high oil and everything to lose from low oil. Back when he was merely an investor, it was fine to listen to his forecasts as he had the ability to move in and out of positions. Now there is no backing out of his wind plan. Pickens' company, Mesa Power, announced a $2 billion investment as the first step in a multi-billion-dollar plan to build the world's largest wind farm in Pampa, Texas. GE has already received the $2 billion order from Pickens and expects another $6 billion in orders from the planned 4,000-megawatt Pampa project alone. GE will begin delivering the turbines in 2010, and current plans call for the project to start producing power in 2011.[3]

Ultimately, Mesa Power plans to have enough turbines to produce 4,000 megawatts of energy. Overall, the Pampa project is expected to cost $10 billion and be completed in 2014. What does history tell us about demand for alternative energy when oil prices drop? The demand for alternative energy drops as well. Any time T. Boone Pickens speaks about oil, his multi-billion-dollar wind turbine purchase needs to be disclosed.

Let's hope that his initiative continues even as the oil bubble bursts. He certainly has our future government on his side. Democratic candidate Barack Obama recently pledged $150 billion over the next decade for affordable, renewable sources of energy that includes solar power, wind power, and the next generation of biofuels. John McCain will be going into greater depth on his plan during this week's Republican National Convention.

A long-term trend away from oil has begun that will send oil speculators running for the hills. The U.S. Commodity Futures Trading Commission released a report showing that four speculators held as much as 81 percent of oil futures contracts in July. There are allegations against Amsterdam-based hedge fund Optiver Holdings that the firm tried to "bully the market" on 19 separate instances by buying large volumes of futures contracts to influence prices. The alleged scheme resulted in a $1 million profit to the defendants. As this manipulation gets cleaned up, I would advise against listening to those in the media with conflicts of interest on oil. The oil bubble will burst in a major way. Buyer beware.[4]

Source: Seeking Alpha, September 3, 2008.

Forget $100 a Barrel—Oil Will Plummet to $30

Remember all those times OPEC tried to tell us that they didn't want high oil prices and we didn't believe them? Well, they meant it. They knew that technology was available to crush oil demand, but they hoped that the low price of oil would keep the technology buried. The cat's now out of the bag. The commodity run is over. The talking heads are trying to temper the recent sell-off in oil by saying that it will settle around $100 a barrel, but that is not what happens when a bubble bursts. Oil is headed back down to historical levels between $30 and $50 a barrel. Consider the following evidence:

1. Oil consumers quickly adjust to high gasoline prices. June data from the IEA reports a 4.7 percent drop in miles driven by Americans year over year. That equals a loss of 12.2 billion road miles of oil demand in just one month. The adjustment has come without a hitch. Staycations have replaced vacations. Honda Civics have replaced Chevy Tahoes.

   Not only are we driving less, we are using less gas while we drive. Everyone was shocked at the gigantic $6.3 billion loss reported in GM's latest earnings announcement. What has happened to automobile demand in just two months is astounding. You have to go through that type of pain only once to never let it happen again. The gas-guzzling SUV market has collapsed overnight. Americans have proven how easy it is to adjust to high oil.

2. New transportation technology has arrived. GM recently announced its goal to have 1,000 hydrogen fuel cell vehicles on California highways by 2014. Honda expects to have 200 Hydrogen FCX Clarities within three years. California is leading the American innovative push with 26 hydrogen fuel stations

already in operation, headlined by Shell's recent opening of the first retail station to sell both gasoline and hydrogen. Of course these numbers are small, but they are extremely significant.[5]

Hybrid numbers started small too. Toyota just announced plans to unveil a new Lexus hybrid and the next generation of its hot-selling Prius next year as the company expects to hit the 1 million mark in hybrid sales by 2010.

3. The next president of the United States will implement alternative energy on a grand scale as never before. John McCain wants to build 45 new nuclear reactors by 2030 and ultimately wants 100 new nuclear plants in the United States. He also proposed a $300 million prize to the auto company that develops a next-generation car battery that will help America become independent from oil.

Barack Obama wants to create a $7,000 tax credit for purchasing advanced vehicles and a mandate that all new vehicles be "flexfuel" by the end of his first term. He also wants to require U.S. utilities to get 25 percent of their electricity from renewable sources like wind and solar.

Oil tycoon T. Boone Pickens has been traveling around the country touting his wind plan. He claims that the Great Plains states are the Saudi Arabia of wind. North Dakota alone has the potential to provide power for a quarter of the country. A Stanford University study found that there is enough wind power to satisfy global demand seven times over—even if only 20 percent of wind power could be captured.[6]

We are also seeing technological breakthroughs in geothermal energy. Raser Technologies can now produce energy from just 180 degree heat through portable mini-power plants. The plan to replace oil is now the top concern of U.S. citizens. Government subsidies will keep the alternative energy trend alive even as oil prices fall.

4. The last piece of evidence for a decline back to historic oil price levels is actually a secret that neither the green people nor the oil people want us to know about. The secret is that new oil is plentiful. Oil drilling rigs are booked until 2012. Recent finds include Brazil, the Gulf of Mexico, and Africa.[7]

The conclusions are obvious. If you are thinking that the drop in oil to $115 a barrel is all we're going to see, then you haven't connected the dots. This oil spike was a bubble fueled by a group of deceived investment speculators who failed to account for adaptable demand destruction from consumers. The technology to replace oil already exists, and high oil prices merely provide the necessary motivation to bring these products to market.

The United States is leading an alternative energy charge that will spread throughout the globe and cause a major shift of power away from the Middle East. I'll save the ramifications of such a power shift for another article, but simply stated, OPEC's greatest fear has been realized. Short oil.

Source: Seeking Alpha, August 15, 2008

The Oil Bubble Will Meet the Same Fate as Tech, Housing

Over the last 10 years, the S&P 500 has returned a meager 2.88 percent. Why? Because in the long run the market doesn't like bubbles. We're now in the third wave of bubble euphoria, and we're hearing the same underlying message that we heard during the first two, just in different terms. During the dot-com era, we watched tech fly to P/E multiples of 200 and above. When fund mangers were questioned about investing in such companies back in 1999, they collectively responded by saying times had changed. Lofty valuations became the new norm—until they crashed, that is. The Nasdaq still isn't even half of what it was in 2000. The market's punishment of the dot-com bubble has lasted for seven years.

Real estate investment shifted into bubble status due to low interest rates and easy lending practices advocated by the Greenspan Federal Reserve. Back in 2005 it was difficult to find anyone who didn't want to jump into real estate. Flipping homes was the new trend for amateurs. Unfortunately it's always the last guys in who get burned by a bubble. Those developers are being suffocated from the holding costs on their sinking investments. After watching home prices double and triple, nationwide home valuations have plunged since 2006 with more yet to come. Home builders and financials have been crushed by the bursting real estate bubble, and it will likely take years before these stocks regain prior highs.

Now it's oil that's bubbling. Two weeks ago oil prices reached a 600 percent increase since the bull market began. The oil bulls are using the same arguments that we heard from tech analysts in 1999 and real estate agents in 2005. They will use any rationale they can find to shift our focus away from the fact that gasoline shortages don't exist and new oil is plentiful. There are now 53 commodity ETFs and ETNs that have caused average daily volumes to soar from 5 million in 2006 to well over 30 million today. History will repeat itself, and the last guys in will get burned. Industry insiders believe that the proper valuation of crude is somewhere between $40 and $50 a barrel. When will this bubble burst? Nobody can predict the exact time, but the essential elements are in place: the Fed is done cutting interest rates, Bush is waiting for Congress to lift the offshore drilling ban, Congress is considering placing limits on speculation, and high gas prices are decreasing demand.

The conclusion is that we are hearing the same story coming from the oil sector that we have heard in previous bubbles. They will tell you that this time is different, or that the fundamentals have changed—when they really haven't. The only thing that has changed is sentiment. This bubble will burst just like the last two, and it will be ugly for those who have gotten caught up in the hype. Over the next six months investors should average in to a short position in the U.S. Oil Fund. Be suspicious of alternative energy as well. Solar, wind, natural gas, etc., . . . will all fall with oil.

Source: Seeking Alpha, July 18, 2008.

The Peak Oil Myth: New Oil Is Plentiful

The data is becoming conclusive that peak oil is a myth. High oil prices are doing their job as oil exploration is flush with new finds:

1. An offshore find by Brazilian state oil company Petrobras in partnership with BG Group and Repsol-YPF may be the world's

biggest discovery in 30 years, the head of the National Petroleum Agency said. A deep-water exploration area could contain as much as 33 billion barrels of oil, an amount that would nearly triple Brazil's reserves and make the offshore bloc the world's third-largest known oil reserve. "This would lay to rest some of the peak oil pronouncements that we were out of oil, that we weren't going to find any more, and that we have to change our way of life," said Roger Read, an energy analyst and managing director at New York–based investment bank Natixis Bleichroeder, Inc.

2. A trio of oil companies led by Chevron Corp. has tapped a petroleum pool deep beneath the Gulf of Mexico that could boost U.S. reserves by more than 50 percent. A test well indicates it could be the biggest new domestic oil discovery since Alaska's Prudhoe Bay a generation ago. Chevron estimated the 300-square-mile region where its test well sits could hold up to 15 billion barrels of oil and natural gas.

3. Kosmos Energy says its oil field at West Cape Three Points is the largest discovery in deep-water West Africa and potentially the largest single field discovery in the region.

4. A new oil discovery has been made by Statoil in the Rag-narrock prospect near the Sleipner area in the North Sea. "It is encouraging that Statoil has made an oil discovery in a little-explored exploration model that is close to our North Sea infra-structure," says Frode Fasteland, acting exploration manager for the North Sea.

5. Shell is currently analyzing and evaluating the well data of their own find in the Gulf of Mexico to determine next steps. This

find is rumored to be capable of producing 100 billion barrels.
Operating in ultradeep waters of the Gulf of Mexico, the Perdido
spar will float on the surface in nearly 8,000 feet of water
and is capable of producing as much as 130,000 barrels of oil
equivalent per day.

6. In Iraq, excavators have struck three oil fields with reserves
   estimated at about 2 billion barrels, Kurdish region's oil minister,
   Ashti Horami, said.

7. Iran has discovered an oil field within its southwest Jofeir oil field
   that is expected to boost Jofeir's oil output to 33,000 barrels per
   day. Iran's new discovery is estimated to have reserves of 750
   million barrels, according to Iran's oil minister, Gholamhossein
   Nozari.

8. The United States holds significant oil shale resources underlying
   a total area of 16,000 square miles. This represents the largest
   known concentration of oil shale in the world and holds an
   estimated 1.5 trillion barrels of oil with 800 billion recoverable
   barrels—enough to meet U.S. demand for oil at current levels
   for 110 years. More than 70 percent of American oil shale is
   on federal land, primarily in Colorado, Utah, and Wyoming.
   In Utah, a developer says his company already has the technology to produce 4,000 barrels a day using a furnace that can
   heat up rock using its own fuel. "This is not a science project,"
   said Daniel G. Elcan, managing director of Oil Shale Exploration Corp. "For many years, the high cost of extracting oil from
   shale exceeded the benefit. But today the calculus is changing,"
   President George Bush said. Senator Orrin Hatch, R-Utah, said

the country has to do everything it can to boost energy production. "We have as much oil in oil shale in Utah, Wyoming, and Colorado as the rest of the world combined," he said.

9. In western North Dakota there is a formation known as the Bakken Shale. The formation extends into Montana and Canada. Geologists have estimated the area holds hundreds of billions of barrels of oil. In an interview provided by the U.S. Geological Survey (USGS), scientist Brenda Pierce put the North Dakota oil in context: "Of the current USGS estimates, this is the largest oil accumulation in the lower 48. It is also the largest continuous type of oil accumulation that we have ever assessed." The USGS study says with today's technology, about 4 billion barrels of oil can be pumped from the Bakken formation. By comparison, the 4 billion barrels in North Dakota represent less than half the oil in the Arctic National Wildlife Refuge, which has an estimated 10 billion barrels of recoverable oil.

The peak oil theory is a moneymaking scam put out by the speculators looking for high commodity returns in a challenging market environment. Most of the above-mentioned finds have occurred in the last two years alone. I didn't even mention the untapped Alaskan oil fields or the recent Danish and Australian finds. In the long term, crude prices will find stability at historic norms because there is no supply problem. How much longer will investors ignore these new oil finds? Probably until they can find other investment alternatives, which won't happen in the broad market until financials stop hemorrhaging. Respect the trend, but understand that this is a bubble preparing to burst. When oil hit its high of $139, it represented more than a 600 percent increase in crude since the bull market began—returns that are eerily similar to the dot-com craze.

There are many theories that sound good but just aren't true. Take Al Gore's global warming crusade. It sounded great, it made perfect sense, but there was just one problem: the facts didn't support it. It seems that the masses who were loudly calling for a global warming crisis have shifted their energies to oil. We are bombarded on a daily basis by those who tell us that we should be fearful. They spin good news into bad. The latest absurdity had Goldman Sachs telling investors that China's 18 percent price increase will actually increase demand! That's a new one. Just like global warming, the rationale for peak oil sounds great, it makes sense, but there is just one small problem: the facts don't support it.

Source: Seeking Alpha, June 22, 2008.

I hope you can extrapolate some lessons from this material and apply them during the next speculative bubble. As a general, stepping-off rule, remember that as soon as the fundamentals no longer match up with the stock price movements, it's all but certain that the high prices will be temporary. An alpha hunter links the past with the present in a way that prepares for the future. When you stay above the sentiment and conventional wisdom of the day, you'll make a lot of money. If you abandon this detached, elevated position, you're likely to go back in time to a prior state of ignorance. The ignorant are the last ones to enter the speculative bubble and end up getting burned.

I've spotted each of the last four bubbles—the dot-com, the housing, the oil, and the bubble of uncertainty—and exploited them by asking the following key questions (I hope that David Frost, Nixon's interviewer, would be proud):

- Have we experienced a price movement that is beyond the historical norm?
- Is this price movement being fueled by investor speculation, or has there truly been a fundamental change in society that explains this spike or fall?
- Are uneducated individuals rushing into the sector?
- Are we seeing extrapolation forecasts that are using data from only the last year to persuade us that this will be a long-term trend?
- Am I in a position to take advantage of the probable consolidations, bankruptcies, and deterioration of asset values that will arrive once this bubble bursts?

If you answer the first four questions in the affirmative, you should employ your corresponding research and come up with a price target for the potential burst. Price targets for a bursting bubble should be aggressive. There is no exact science that forecasts the rise and fall of bubbles, but common sense suggests that bubbles will result in a pullback of anywhere between 60 to 80 percent. Bespoke Investment Group reported that the bursting of the housing bubble was quite similar to the bursting of the dot-com bubble. They report that the bursting of the Nasdaq lasted 647 trading days with declines of 78.29 percent, while the bursting of the home-builder bubble lasted 750 trading days with declines of 67 percent in the S&P 1500 Homebuilder Index. If you think that those numbers are similar, the growth numbers of the two bubbles are so aligned as to be eerie. Both bubbles rose for exactly the same number of days: 2,000. The home builders' rose 839 percent during their 2000s' bubble, and the Nasdaq rose 640 percent during its 1990s' bubble.[8]

The oil bubble, on the other hand, set some new precedents. The size of its rise and fall compares with the others, but the timeline occurred in hyperspeed. On December 19, 2008, Bespoke reported that when oil hit its peak of $145.29 in July 2008, it had risen 770 percent from its low of $16.70 in 2001; by the time the report was issued, it had sunk 76.1 percent beneath the peak. While other bubbles took years to explode, this one was over and done in five months.[9]

Option LEAPS are the ultimate investment vehicle to take advantage of bubbles. Investors can maximize their potential when they purchase out-of-the-money calls or puts at the designated future price target. You should know right now that it is extremely difficult to profit from both sides of the trade. How high the bubble will go is impossible to predict—only the bursting is guaranteed. I would much rather be invested on the bursting side than risk being along for the momentum ride that could leave me looking like a fool who was last out the door. Buying an out-of-the-money put at a strike price 70 percent down from the peak of the Nasdaq, housing, or oil bubbles would have cost you relatively nothing at the time. An oil put at the $40 strike price could have been purchased for 0.50 in July 2008. By December 2008, those options were trading at 10.00.

A Bubble from Antiquity

Although this has been the decade of the bubble, they've crept into economies before. A particularly interesting one occurred in the 1630s in Holland, during the Dutch Golden Age. This is a story I grew up with, courtesy of my maternal grandfather Duvalois. He emigrated from Holland in the 1950s, knowing no English and without job prospects. Nevertheless, he and his wife Dina believed in the American Dream and made the best of things. They brought with them the legend of the tulip, which for them wasn't always a thing of beauty. In the service Grandpa sometimes had to eat tulip bulbs, and he threatened his grandkids with the same treatment if they didn't clean their dinner plates!

The classic *Extraordinary Popular Delusions and the Madness of Crowds*, compiled by Charles Mackay in 1841, relates the fascinating story of the seventeenth-century Dutch "tulipomania." Introduced to the nation in the fifteenth century, this flower became a coveted luxury item and a status symbol among the Dutch elite. The tulip bulbs would grow flowers with vivid colors, lines, and flames on the petals. Growers gave their new varieties exalted titles like "admiral" or "general." Tulips can be propagated through both seeds and buds. Seed from a tulip will form a flowering bulb in 7 to 12 years. The cultural appeal of tulips was so great that it created a booming market for the bulbs.

The Dutch at this time were at the vanguard of finance, and they were eager to introduce consumers to new markets. They even allowed short selling of tulip bulbs until it was banned in 1636. In 1634, in large part because of the increasing demand for the new varieties in France, speculators began to enter this market. By

1636, the tulip futures market was soaring. There are documented accounts of a man offering 12 acres of land for one rare bulb and of 40 bulbs being traded for 100,000 Dutch guilders—this at a time when a skilled laborer earned 150 guilders a year. Many who played the tulip market became instantaneously rich. Everyone imagined that the passion for tulips would last forever and that the wealthy from every part of the world would pay whatever prices were asked for them. Nobles, citizens, farmers, mechanics, seamen, footmen, maidservants, and even chimney sweeps dabbled in tulips.

By February 1637, tulip traders could no longer find new buyers willing to pay increasingly inflated prices for their bulbs. As you might guess, the demand for tulips collapsed, and prices plummeted—the speculative bubble had burst. The panicked tulip speculators sought help from the government of the Netherlands, which responded by declaring that anyone who had bought contracts to purchase bulbs in the future could void their contract by paying a 10 percent fee. Attempts to placate all the losers among the buyers and speculators were unsuccessful. The mania finally ended, Mackay says, with people stuck with the bulbs they held at the end of the crash—no court decreed that contracts were enforceable because it was judged that the debts had been accumulated in a process not unlike gambling.[10]

So you see that bubbles have a long history. For better or worse, it's an ongoing phenomenon. The alpha investor knows this and stays prepared.

eight

CRISIS INVESTING

Red Cross for the Investor

Crises occur randomly and disrupt the cyclical flow of the economy. It is imperative that investors prepare to handle such conditions before they arise. I define an investment crisis as an event that occurs as the result of a military, economic, political, environmental, or social emergency that produces a negative unwind within a sector. The cause and effect between emergencies and crises is not inevitable; emergency events do not necessarily result in investment crisis situations. In fact, most quick-hitting surprises that do not originate in a vital sector of the market have a minimal impact.

The year 2005 brought us the Hurricane Katrina disaster that put 80 percent of New Orleans under water, killed 1,836 people, and caused over $100 billion in damages. It was the costliest tropical cyclone in U.S. history. In addition to the damages, the federal government received withering criticism for what many regarded as its tardy, ineffectual response. You'd think that if ever there were an environmental crisis with the power to derail the market, this would be it. When the country began to anticipate the storm, on August 23, the Dow Jones Industrial Average was at 10,519. When Katrina hit the mainland on August 29, the Dow was at 10,463, and two weeks later it was at 10,678. Hurricane Katrina brought about many tragedies, but it didn't even put a dent in the index.[1]

How about 9/11? The most devastating terrorist attack in our history, it forced Americans into the awareness that we are never completely safe. This realization did wreak havoc on the stock market in the short run, but its long-term impact proved to be a positive, just as most wars are. On Monday, September 10, 2001, the Dow ended at 9,605, and then the market closed for the rest of the week following the attacks. The market reopened for business the following Monday about 300 points down and closed the day at 8,920. The market low came on Friday of the same week; investor fear climaxed, and the Dow finished at 8,235, representing a two-week drop of 14.3 percent. Yet, by October 2 the Dow already had crawled back above 9,000, and by December 5 it was above 10,000. What this demonstrates is that the market tends to respond relatively well to crisis events outside of its financial realm.[2]

But if the crisis occurs *inside* the realm, watch out. In this case, a troubled market variable like currency, credit, or consumer confidence may end up communicating its symptoms to the rest of the economy. In the 1970s the United States experienced an inflationary crisis that put the market into a multiyear rut from which it didn't recover until the Reagan Revolution. Then we had the savings and loan (S&L) crises in the late 1980s and early 1990s that resulted in the failure of 745 S&L associations. The turmoil that was kicked up in the finance industry and the real estate market contributed heavily to the 1990 to 1991 economic recession and a nine-month Dow sell-off of 15.1 percent. Most recently, the financial sector crisis of 2007 to 2009 resulted in a 55 percent drop in the Dow index in 18 months. In each case, the initial crisis sent shivers through the investing world and ultimately across the globe. No industry escaped its wrath. The broad market could not recover until the financials returned to health.

When the time of crisis comes, investors need to have a system of coping, assessment, operation, and recovery. Very likely, they'll draw off the lessons of events in their own lives. When I think of the word *crisis*, I'm transported back to January 17, 1994, when my bed started shaking at 4:30 A.M. as if somebody was jumping up and down on the mattress. My first reaction was to find out who it was and go after them. I jumped off the bed and looked around the best I could in the dark but couldn't find anybody. As I groped about, I realized that the floor was shaking as well. After a few seconds, dishes began shattering on the floor in the kitchen, voices were screaming from upstairs, and literally everything around me seemed to be on the verge of tumbling into chaos. That's what it feels like to be one town over from the epicenter of a 6.7-magnitude earthquake. This one killed 72 people, injured over 9,000 people, and caused an estimated $20 billion in damages in the Los Angeles area. It was awful to drive through the city and see houses, an apartment building, and a hospital in ruins. I remember one particular street where the tremors seemed to have skipped over every other house; one would be untouched while those on either side were reduced to rubble.

After living through that incident, I made sure to get up to speed on the latest in emergency preparedness, and I have been active in my community response teams ever since. Here too I want to be clear that I'm not making a case for the equivalence between investing challenges and matters of life and death. I am saying, however, that you can develop a crisis response strategy in life that you can also apply effectively when your money is on the line. As we walk through the steps, we're going to revisit the scene of the recent financial crisis and subsequent reactions to it.

A Crisis Response Strategy

Step 1: Survey the Scene

The large-scale environmental tragedies like earthquakes and fires are easy to see, but some of the others arrive quietly, such as a flu pandemic. The media provide vital advance warnings in these cases, while the tragic implications develop over time. Our job is to monitor the warnings carefully without losing our cool. Over-reaction has its own dangers. It's a good idea to have a list of crisis catalysts that could be on the horizon.

We heard the first murmurs about the financial crisis in October 2007. It was reported that Citigroup and JPMorgan Chase were working with the Treasury Department to come up with a $75 billion structured investment vehicle (SIV) fund to bail out the banks carrying an excess of these securities that were rapidly losing value in the housing market downturn. The mortgage-backed securities that were tied to subprime loans were seen as especially toxic.

At this early stage, an investor had to ask some critical questions that probably seem more obvious now than they were then: What are SIVs? Why do banks need to be bailed out? Why is the government getting involved?

By December 2007 the banks and Treasury Secretary Hank Paulson had decided that their $75 billion superfund backstop solution for the SIV market wasn't going to be enough to get the job done. They quickly realized that they couldn't come up with enough private sector funds to do what they felt was needed. That was a very bad sign. Once we knew that the private sector had no solution, it became clear that our fate was going to be dictated by the actions of the government. And history shows us that the government usually will hit and miss a few times before they get it right.[3]

Step 2: Determine the Root Cause

Treating the symptoms of the crisis will only prolong it. The root cause must be identified and fixed for the market to recover. Just as it's difficult to see the truth in the midst of a bubble, it's also difficult to see the truth in the midst of a crisis. All parties involved will seek to deflect blame and accountability. The various conflicts of interest will spin rationale upside down until nobody knows how we ended up in the crisis in the first place. I find it interesting that the scholars can never decide what caused the Great Depression or what caused the double-digit inflation of the 1970s. Even the scholars get turned around in the endless debate.

Common sense alone will lead you to the root cause. It was no different during the financial crisis of 2008. The general opinion in the media was that this correction in real estate was so severe that it was causing balance sheet stress among financial institutions that hadn't occurred since the 1930s. I judged this general opinion to be bizarre because I recalled that we had experienced multiple real estate corrections throughout history without similar panic. These balance sheet woes were causing all lending to dry up. This lack of funding caused corporations to tighten their own spending, and it caused a broad-based consumer spending slowdown as the entire economy became paralyzed by the unknown damages caused by these SIVs. So I framed the question: Why was the balance sheet pressure in this real estate correction so much more severe than in the other corrections we had survived? The answer led me to the root cause.

It wasn't easy, of course, because everyone had an opinion, and it was hard to concentrate in the din. The government wanted to blame the crisis on the newfound greed of corporate executives, whose companies took advantage of ignorant consumers by allowing them to buy homes they couldn't afford. Since the banks had grown rich during this era of unqualified lending, it was easy to lay the blame squarely on the shoulders of Countrywide Financial, Wachovia, Bank of America, Citigroup, Bear Stearns, and Lehman Brothers, all of which had recorded major profits while handling these bad debt obligations. Because 2008 was an election year, the campaign rhetoric was continuous, and it contained plenty of disparaging remarks about the big, bad, greedy banks. All the candidates were bellowing that it was time for government to clean up the mess on Wall Street with stricter regulation and increased transparency. Wall Street, always derided as greedy, was now a shady place as well. It was too easy to paint this picture, especially when the late-night comics jumped into the act: "More bad news from President Bush. Remember those rebate checks from a few months ago? He wants them back. We need to give that money to rich people on Wall Street. They need it more than you do."

Or from 2009: "President Obama, getting very tough now, has imposed a $500,000 salary cap for executives getting federal bailout money. And, listen to this: Now on weekends, they can only play miniature golf. No more 18 holes."[4]

It was such an easy story line to remember that people accepted it almost unthinkingly. For me, though, it didn't provide an answer to my initial question. The high salaries of corporate executives and even the issuance of toxic subprime loans weren't enough to cause the collapse we were seeing in the financial sector. The politicians and the media mapped out the symptoms in detail, but they failed to pinpoint the root cause.

Clearly, the stress originated from one element of government regulation that required immediate capital to be raised each time a bank reported a write-down. This regulation of urgency, called mark-to-market (MTM) accounting, received almost no media coverage for 18 months. Banks were taking write-downs at an unprecedented rate because the market for their debt securities temporarily had shut down. Instead of recognizing that this illiquid securities market was only a short-term glitch, the regulatory requirements forced the banks to raise new capital to supplement those losses in a rigid form of mark-to-market accounting.

This put banks in a bad double bind. They were being forced to immediately raise capital at a time when there was no private capital to be raised. Why didn't this same crippling phenomenon happen in previous real estate corrections? Because the mark-to-market regulation was instituted in November 2007. This was a *new* regulatory environment that did not allow banks to wait out the housing recovery.

To understand this, let's go back to the analogy of furs in summertime. Imagine that you bought a fur coat for $20,000, and the following summer you could fetch only $5,000 for it because you were trying to unload it in 100 degree weather. No worries: you expect that kind of short-term devaluation. The real injustice—and illogic—comes when you find out that you are required to raise $15,000 to supplement that August write-down! It's one thing to force someone to assign value to fur coats in August; it's quite another to ask that person to raise capital because that value is so far below the purchase price.

This is what mark-to-market accounting demanded of the banks. It was not without a worthy purpose because it gave investors a current glimpse at bank balance sheet valuations, but it crossed the line into utter ridiculousness when the regulators required capital to be raised in the short run. Beginning in November 2007, the stock market became a playground for a group of day traders because of this new obsession with short-term marks. Until the absurdity of the situation was identified and corrected, there could be no end to the crisis. At last the root cause was identified.

Step 3: Research Solutions

As I was discussing the root cause of the financial crisis with my colleagues on TheStreet.com, a fellow columnist, Jeff Miller, showed me the idea being presented by former FDIC Chairman Bill Isaac. Throwing capital at the problem wasn't working because the thirst for capital within the system was unquenchable. A change in regulation was the only thing that could save the remaining banks from failure. Read the following excerpt from Isaac's testimony before Congress on March 12, 2009, which summarizes his opinion of the crisis:

Fair value (mark-to-market) accounting is highly pro-cyclical; when things are going great, it pours more gasoline on the fire; but when things are going poorly, it really causes banks and financial institutions to take excessive losses as they "mark things to market" in a climate where there IS NO MARKET! Banks and financial institutions have been taking excessive write-downs. MTM accounting has destroyed well over $500 billion of capital in our financial system. Because banks are able to lend up to 10 times their capital, MTM accounting has also destroyed over $5 trillion of lending capacity, contributing significantly to a severe credit contraction and an economic downturn that has cost millions of jobs and wiped out vast amounts of retirement savings on which millions of people were counting. Taxpayers have been called upon to invest in our financial institutions to help repair the damage caused by MTM accounting. Congress has authorized $700 billion, and the FDIC is now asking for up to $500 billion more. I believe firmly that if the SEC and FASB had suspended this MTM rule nine months ago—in favor of marking these assets to their true economic values based on actual and projected cash flows—our financial system and economy would not be in anywhere near the crisis that they are in today.

I was Chairman of the FDIC during the banking crisis of the 1980s. The problems in the U.S. financial system in the 1980s, despite what we are hearing from some government leaders and the media, were more serious than we are facing thus far today. One of the many problems we faced during the 1980s was the massive insolvency of thrift institutions (that is, savings banks insured by the FDIC and S&Ls insured by the former Federal Savings & Loan Insurance Corporation) due to their holdings of long-term, fixed-rate mortgages and bonds during a time of very high interest rates. Ironically, MTM accounting had surface appeal to me during this period, as I thought it might in the future force banks and thrifts to keep the maturities of their assets and liabilities in better balance.

I asked the FDIC staff to consider whether we should push for MTM accounting, and we solicited comments and studied the issue for the better part of a year. We rejected MTM accounting for three principal reasons. The underlying economic problems of the 1980s in the United States were more serious than the economic problems confronting us this time around—at least so far. The prime rate exceeded 21 percent, and the economy plunged into a deep recession in 1981 to 1982, with the agricultural sector in a depression. Unemployment approached 11 percent. These economic problems led to massive problems in the banking and thrift industries. The savings bank industry was more than $100 billion insolvent if we had valued it on a market basis, and the S&L industry was in similar condition. A bubble burst in the energy sector, and a rolling real estate recession hit one region after another.

Continental Illinois (the seventh largest bank) failed, many of the large regional banks went down (including 9 of the 10 largest banks in Texas), and hundreds of farm banks failed, as did an even larger number of thrifts. Three thousand banks and thrifts failed from 1980 through 1991, and many others went out of business through mergers. It could have been much worse. The money center banks were loaded up with third world debt that was valued in the markets at cents on the dollar. If we had marked those loans to market prices, virtually every one of our money center banks would have been insolvent. We instead marked them to our estimate of their true economic value. The current worldwide crisis in the financial system demonstrates conclusively that major principles of accounting are much too important to be left solely to accountants. Accounting standards today are set by the FASB, a five-member board that is shrouded in mystery. The SEC has authority to overrule the FASB for public companies, but it almost never does—at least not publicly. The result is a system of accounting that is not accountable.

You will no doubt hear from the SEC and FASB that you should not politicize the process of setting accounting standards. I agree with that general proposition, although it is difficult to resist political action when the SEC and FASB are sitting on their hands in the midst of a worldwide financial crisis they played such a large role in creating. I believe a board along the lines suggested in H.R. 1349 will ensure that not only will we approach accounting standards with objectivity, we will bring to bear the vast experience of those who are charged with maintaining a strong economy and financial system.

We had mark-to-market accounting in the 1930s, and finally eight years into the Depression in the 1930s, the government, President Roosevelt, and the Secretary of Treasury said, "Why can't we get out of the Depression?" And mark-to-market accounting is one of the key things they identified that was keeping us from getting out of the Depression, and they abandoned it in favor of historical cost accounting, which we used for the next 50 years or so, 50 or 60 years, until the SEC decided to go back to mark-to-market accounting over the objections of the Secretary of the Treasury, the Chairman of the Fed, and the Chairman of the FDIC.[5]

Step 4: Determine Who Is Affected by the Root Cause

In response to the balance sheet pressure caused by MTM, our banks stopped lending to one another, they stopped lending to businesses, and they stopped lending to consumers. The private equity market dried up. Consumer loans for education, automobiles, and homes became impossible to secure. The London LIBOR went through the roof. This particular root cause was affecting the banks primarily, but as in most crises, the symptoms were spreading throughout the global economy as well.

The defining moment occurred on September 15, 2008, when Lehman Brothers declared bankruptcy. In the first half of 2008, Lehman stock had lost 73 percent of its value as credit markets continued to tighten and Lehman's large exposure to lower-rated mortgage-backed securities caused it to write down billions of dollars from its balance sheet. Until a solution was put in place, the hedge funds were enjoying a short selling feeding frenzy on bank after bank, and Lehman was an easy target.

It was unfathomable to most observers that Lehman, a financial services leader since 1850, could be beaten down by the short sellers in response to Lehman's immediate capital needs, but it was happening before our very eyes. Immediately following the bankruptcy filing, an already distressed financial sector began a period of extreme volatility during which the Dow experienced its largest one-day point loss, largest intra-day range (more than 1,000 points), and largest daily point gain in history. In the wake of Lehman's sinking, all other financial institutions that were threatened by large write-downs became easy downside targets for investors.[6]

It also became clear that the damage would not be limited to the financial sector. The loss of confidence spread to all sectors of the economy; there were no safe havens.

Step 5: Wait Patiently for the Solution

For 18 months the market was unable to rally because of weak financials. Where would we be if mark to market had been altered at the first signs of the crisis? The answer to that question will make you want to throw up: None of the so-called troubled banks would have been forced to close their doors, none of the taxpayer-funded bailouts would have been needed, Bear Stearns, Lehman Brothers, Freddie Mac, Fannie Mae, AIG, Washington Mutual, Wachovia, Merrill Lynch, and others would still be operating as private, stand-alone institutions, and all of their employees would still have jobs. Our stock market would never have sold off 55 percent the way it did; it probably would have sold off a more typical 5 to 15 percent, and the huge surge in fear that led to the freeze in credit and the collapse of consumer spending would have amounted to little more than a few tremors. To be sure, 2008 still would have been a bad year, but it wouldn't have been anything like it was. Investors would not have had to tap their reserves of patience anywhere near as often as they have.

The mark-to-market regulation was the biggest economic blunder in a generation at least. Anything short of altering this law didn't do us any good. Once MTM was altered, the way was paved for the stock market recovery. Private equity could resume operations. Lending could expand. The way was paved for housing and unemployment stabilization. If you're still looking for what triggered this recession, look no further than November 2007, when mark-to-market accounting was implemented. If you want to pick a triggering event for the recovery, I'd suggest the ending of MTM in April 2009. Our own regulators caused this crisis. Unintended consequences of government regulation have played a huge role in the changes to the stock market.

The former chairman of the SEC, Christopher Cox, was a key economic leader during 2008, and his decisions deserve intense scrutiny. From his first day at work at the SEC, Cox was concerned with increasing investor transparency. His first initiative was to create new rules requiring the mutual fund industry to make their prospectuses easier for investors to read, understand, and access. Cox vigorously defended the 2002 Sarbanes-Oxley Act even though its many unintended consequences were hurting American business. The accounting compliance costs associated with implementing the SOX transparency requirements were so outrageous that hundreds of companies left the United States. These costs in fact were much higher than even the SEC had predicted, but Cox consented only to minor changes. In June 2007 the commission voted unanimously to repeal the uptick rule. Cox waited until September 17, 2008, to enforce the rule against naked short selling. In an interview with the *Washington Post*, Cox infuriated investors everywhere when he claimed, "What we have done in this current turmoil is stay calm, which has been our greatest contribution—not being impulsive, not changing the rules willy-nilly, but going through a very professional and orderly process that takes into account unintended consequences and gives ample notice to market participants."[7]

At last Cox was forced to look into the MTM problem by the Emergency Economic Stabilization Act. If it weren't for an urgent request from Congress, I doubt he ever would have revisited the issue. In his own words, "Our ongoing study on mark-to-market accounting is mandated by the Emergency Economic Stabilization Act, signed into law earlier this month. Under the terms of the act, it will be completed by January 2, 2009. We are working on this study, as the statute requires, in close consultation with the Secretary of Treasury and the Board of Governors of the Federal Reserve System, whose representatives are with us today as observers."[8]

While the regulators were asleep at the wheel, Treasury Secretary Hank Paulson was busy working on his faulty solution at the expense of the U.S. taxpayer. As soon as he realized in December 2007 that the $75 billion SIV fund wasn't going to be enough to support the $14 trillion mortgage industry, he tried to incite fear in the marketplace as a means to get Congress to approve his emergency bailout package. I believe that the fear mongering was a preplanned tactic set to be employed in September 2008. Naked short selling hadn't been banned and neither had mark-to-market accounting. Paulson could have stopped the Lehman bankruptcy process, but he didn't. He needed a terrifying event to keep people from recognizing that economic conditions really weren't that bad. He needed to orchestrate fear. Wall Street had gotten into a dangerous habit during the last month of each quarter—the time period I call the "quarterly dead zone"—of acting like the world was coming to an end because of all the uncertainty in financials. Paulson used September 2008 to his perceived advantage.

The real data showed the following:

- Unemployment was little more than 6 percent, compared with 25 percent during a real depression.
- Yearly GDP growth was over 3 percent compared with a 25 percent contraction during a real depression.
- Consumer prices were still rising, compared with a 30 percent fall during a real depression.
- Only 4 percent of mortgages were delinquent compared with 40 percent during a real depression.
- Fewer than 20 banks had failed over the past couple of years compared with 9,000 during a real depression.[9]

Despite all of these positive data points, the stock market was pricing itself as if a depression was coming. Paulson knew that the end-of-the-world mentality would return in September, and he was intent on turning the panic into a long-term solution for the mortgage market. The proposed bailout plan wasn't a bailout at all; the term was employed in service of the goal of inciting panic. The plan really is a superfund that will act as a mortgage security specialist to provide confidence and liquidity during housing cycles. Its ability to buy and hold these beaten-down assets, and hopefully turn a profit over time, would help its legislation become part of a permanent solution.

Unfortunately, the whole thing worked like a giant head fake on investors. The market continued to tank for another four months after Paulson got his $700 billion in TARP funding. The fear that he stirred up to pressure Congress into giving him his money spread to Main Street USA, and consumers stopped buying. Consumer spending in the fourth quarter of 2008 experienced its worst drop in over 25 years. Patience and calm were critical investor attributes as the government failed over and over to solve the crisis. Many investment advisors were eager to call for a market bottom but until the root cause was solved, there would be no bottom.

Step 6: Implement a Strategy of Safety

As you await a solution to the root cause of the crisis, you must adapt your style to fit the current conditions. Investment strategy during the financial crisis was very simple. The economic data was obviously worsening, so it was time to follow the rules for a worsening economy that I outlined in Chapter 5. Puts should have been owned on the sector that was leading the economy down; that sector was obviously financials. In January 2008 the financial ETF (XLF) was priced at $25 a share. A 2010 LEAPS $25 put could have been purchased at that time for 3.00. A year later it would have been worth 18.00. Not a bad return. Would owning that put have helped your portfolio?

Step 7: After the Solution, Forecast the Long-Term Ramifications

On April 2, 2009, the FASB at last voted to alter mark to market. The primary change in the rules relates to how management defines an asset on the balance sheet. Under the old rules, an asset defined as "other than temporarily impaired" triggered a write-down in value that impacted earnings and may have caused reserve capital to fall below regulatory requirements. Management can now avoid the classification by asserting that the company had the intent and ability to retain the asset on the balance sheet until the valuation recovered. The new rules will allow management to avoid the classification by stating that the management "intend to hold the asset and that it is more likely than not that they will," which is a reduced standard. Furthermore, only losses related to the underlying creditworthiness would affect earnings and regulatory capital. Losses attributed to market conditions would be disclosed elsewhere.[10]

After the solution was in place, President Obama wanted to put his own stamp on the situation and take some credit for eliminating the greed on Wall Street. He zeroed in on executive compensation. It tapped into one of the deepest pools of popular disgust. It was easy to be angered by the ludicrous executive compensation packages that were getting paid out even in the midst of the crisis. Can you believe that Citigroup CEO Vikram Pandit earned $38 million in salary and stock even as his company lost $27.7 billion in 2008 and stayed solvent only because of a $45 billion government bailout? He wasn't the alone. Goldman Sachs CEO Lloyd Blankfein topped the CEO earnings charts after making $42.9 million. A year earlier, executive compensation was even more out of whack. It wasn't uncommon to hear that some CEO made over $100 million. This era is over. None of these executives built their companies. They are merely stewards of a publicly held institution. I don't think anyone feels that these CEOs deserve to be treated like royalty. Do shareholders really get more expertise out of these guys by paying them $100 million? What if they got paid only $10 million? Warren Buffett pays himself a salary of $175,000 a year to run Berkshire Hathaway. President Obama gets paid $450,000 to do his job.

Buffett, 78, has criticized boards of directors for acceding to CEO demands for multi-million-dollar compensation packages: "Half of the directors I've met on corporate boards don't know anything about business. They are not going to do anything that not only gets them kicked off that board but that reduces their chances of getting on another one." What happens next will just be one of the ramifications of the financial crisis.[11]

To lay out the specifics of Obama's plan for the financial sector, I will provide you with some excerpts from a landmark speech he gave on April 14, titled "A New Foundation":

> I want every American to know that each action we take and each policy we pursue is driven by a larger vision of America's future—a future where sustained economic growth creates good jobs and rising incomes; a future where prosperity is fueled not by excessive debt, reckless speculation, and fleeing profit, but is instead built by skilled, productive workers; by sound investments that will spread opportunity at home and allow this nation to lead the world in the technologies, innovations, and discoveries that will shape the twenty-first century. That is the America I see. That is the future I know we can have.

> And by the way, one of the changes that I'd like to see, and I'm going to be talking about this in the weeks to come: It's once again seeing our best and our brightest commit themselves to making things. Engineers, scientists, innovators. For so long, we have placed at the top of our pinnacle folks who can manipulate numbers. And engage in complex financial calculations. And that's good, we need some of that. But you know, what we could use are some more scientists and engineers who are building and making things that we can export to other countries.

All of these actions—the Recovery Act, the bank capitalization program, the housing plan, the strengthening of the non-bank credit market, the auto plan, and our work at the G20—have been necessary pieces of the recovery puzzle. They have been designed to increase aggregate demand, get credit flowing again to families and businesses, and help them ride out the storm.

It is simply not sustainable to have a twenty-first-century financial system that is governed by twentieth-century rules and regulations that allowed the recklessness of a few to threaten the entire economy. It is not sustainable to have an economy where in one year, 40 percent of our corporate profits came from a financial sector that was based too much on inflated home prices, maxed out credit cards, overleveraged banks, and overvalued assets; or an economy where the incomes of the top 1 percent have skyrocketed while the typical working household has seen their income decline by nearly $2,000.

For as some were chasing ever-bigger bonuses and short-term profits over the last decade, we continued to neglect the long-term threats to our prosperity: the crushing burden that the rising cost of health care is placing on families and businesses; the failure of our education system to prepare our workers for a new age; the progress that other nations are making on clean energy industries and technologies while we remain addicted to foreign oil; the growing debt that we're passing on to our children. And even after we emerge from the current recession, these challenges will still represent major obstacles that stand in the way of our success in the twenty-first century.

There is a parable at the end of the Sermon on the Mount that tells the story of two men. The first built his house on a pile of sand, and it was destroyed as soon as the storm hit. But the second is known as the wise man, for when "the rain descended, and the floods came, and the winds blew, and beat upon that house, . . . , it fell not: for it was founded upon a rock."

We cannot rebuild this economy on the same pile of sand. We must build our house upon a rock. We must lay a new foundation for growth and prosperity—a foundation that will move us from an era of borrow and spend to one where we save and invest; where we consume less at home and send more exports abroad.[12]

Obama's agenda is helping to fuel the dynamic of a new Wall Street. Investors should pay particular attention to stock float, where one can observe direct effects of the quasi-nationalization of banks that occurred late in the crisis. The government exchanged bailout funds for preferred shares, which were then turned into common stock. There are profound unintended consequences when there is a change in the number of shares outstanding and the resulting float.

Take Citigroup as an example, an institution that is right in the middle of this phenomenon. Less float means more directional velocity. If the direction for financials is heading up, the 36 percent stake by the U.S. government in Citigroup will put additional upside pressure on the stock. Not good for shorts, very good for the long-side speculators.

It is expected that Citi will exchange $27.5 billion in preferred shares for common stock and that the U.S. government will tender up to $25 billion of its preferred holdings into common stock. This scenario would give the government a 36 percent stake in the company, and it would increase the number of shares outstanding from the current 5.5 billion to anywhere between 13 billion and

21 billion, depending on how many investors participate. This dilution is positive for Citi because its tangible common equity will rise to approximately $81 billion, up from $30 billion at the beginning of 2009.

Of course, with all of this dilution, Citi is at risk of becoming a stock that is virtually impossible to move because of the ridiculous amount of shares outstanding. However, recently the company announced that it will seek shareholder and government approval to execute a reverse split, with a range anywhere from 1-for-2 to 1-for-30. This move makes a lot of sense for Citi. It's looking like they may end up with a total number of shares outstanding below the current 5.5 billion; the amount could end up lower than 1 billion.

Until now, most have viewed the government stake as a negative for the stock, but that perception might change quickly. A float of less than 1 billion, with 36 percent of it stable, isn't so negative in the wake of a crisis. The government won't be selling, and most other investors who have ridden this stock down to its depths won't be selling either. It is conceivable that 80 percent of the shares outstanding won't be sold in the near term, which leaves a float of only 20 percent for investors to buy and sell. Many firms try to manipulate their stock prices by restricting the percentage of tradable float. According to a research report released by Robin Greenwood of Harvard Business School, "Prices rise when the float is contracted and fall when the float is released."[13]

Don't let a crisis get you down. The liquidity of stock ownership allows us to function throughout the rough patches. Be grateful that we can sell and reposition our portfolios in response to the changes. This isn't like investing in real estate where your holdings are impossible to move in a crisis situation. As we continue to recover from the financial crisis, unforeseen investment opportunities will surely arise. Alan Greenspan summed it up nicely: "Crisis, at least for a while, destabilizes the relationships that characterize normal, functioning markets. It creates opportunities to reap abnormally high profits in the buying and selling of some goods, services, and assets. The scramble by market participants to seize those opportunities presses prices, exchange rates, and interest rates back to market-appropriate levels and thereby eliminates both the abnormal profit margins and the inefficiencies that create them."

nine

CASE STUDY: A TECH REVOLUTION POISED FOR TAKEOFF

The paths that information takes through our world have been growing steadily more sophisticated and fluid—in effect, shorter—since the advent of the Internet, but we're just getting started. The revolution kicked off in cyberspace is bringing people in other hemispheres into our offices and living rooms and creating a neighborhood that is truly global. It's been going on for 15 years now, and that's long enough for many to assume that our society already has absorbed the full impact of these changes. Nothing could be further from the truth. Until 3G and 4G wireless access reach the masses, this tech revolution won't even have exited the toddler stage. Everything you've seen so far is just a warm-up. Geographical distinctions will continue to diminish as we connect to foreign citizens and business in new ways.

Speed means everything. Google Vice President Marissa Mayer recently spoke at the Web 2.0 conference and shared a bit of what her company has learned about speed, the user experience, and user satisfaction. She began with a story about a recent user test Google conducted. A group of Google searchers were asked how many search results they wanted to see. Users asked for more, a lot more than the 10 results Google normally displays. More is more, they said. So, as a test Google, increased the number of search results to 30. Traffic and revenue from Google searchers in the experimental group dropped by 20 percent. Ouch. Why, when users had asked for this, did they seem to hate it? After a bit of detective work, Mayer explained, they found an uncontrolled variable. The page with 10 results took 0.4 second to generate. The page with 30 results took 0.9 second. Half a second delay caused a dip in user satisfaction and a 20 percent drop in traffic. This conclusion may be surprising—people notice a half second delay?— but it was confirmed at Amazon.com as well. In A/B tests, they tried delaying the page in increments of 100 milliseconds and found that even very small delays resulted in substantial and costly drops in revenue.

As Mayer said, "Users really respond to speed." She described how a new version of Google Maps had been rolled out that was lighter (in page size) and rendered much faster. Google Maps immediately saw substantial boosts in traffic and usage. If people do not like to wait, Google realized, you can't let them.[1]

Each time a new technology is able to break down another societal barrier through enhanced communication, you can expect an adrenaline shot to the economic system. A more unified population is a more productive population. Increased freedom invigorates capitalism. However, a flourishing economy doesn't happen overnight. It can take a few decades for new technology to fundamentally change society.

On May 1, 1893, the greatest spectacle of electricity yet seen occurred at the Columbian Exposition in Chicago. President Grover Cleveland pushed a button, and a hundred thousand lamps burst into light. An orchestra played Handel's "Hallelujah Chorus," and the observing crowds cheered as electrically operated fountains threw water skyward and cannons boomed. This was the new "City of Light," the city of the future. The sight so dazzled author L. Frank Baum that he was inspired to create the Emerald City in his book *The Wizard of Oz*. It was a glorious display of a resource that was just beginning to reshape the society that had created it. However, it would take much more time for industry to harness the full power of electricity and produce a full-on transformation in the nation's lifestyle.[2]

The U.S. transportation system underwent a similar, gradual transformation. America had a system of turnpikes and roads throughout most of the 1800s, but it took decades for the system to have a measurable impact on commerce and trade. The first roads were muddy, slow, and unsafe. Once speed and security were improved along the highways and the right vehicles were developed, the network delivered profound economic benefits to the cities it connected. Land sales boomed in newly accessible areas, settlement and agricultural development proceeded rapidly, and the geographical reach of competition increased exponentially. The country was no longer a sprawling collection of isolated townships.[3]

Both electricity and roads enjoyed an initial stage of enthusiasm and awe before settling into a long, tedious process of implementation and improvement. But in both cases, the intermediate stage was followed by an even bigger wave of enthusiasm that proved to be both hugely profitable and long lasting. I see the Internet developing along the exact same pattern. The dot-com craze that hit in 1999 was the first bloom of excitement; the crash was the first hiccup. The enthusiasm was warranted but premature. The second wave seems likely to hit in the decade after 2010, and it will far surpass anything we hoped for 10 years ago.

This time around, even the government is getting into the game. In 2009 Vivek Kundra was appointed to be the first-ever chief information officer of the United States. President Obama created this position in acknowledgment of the technological revolution we are living in.

Until now, much of the data that our central agencies compile has remained secret and inaccessible. It got to the point where the federal government was operating 24,000 Web sites in incompatible or obsolete formats. Piles of important data were left to languish. Kundra's task is to change all that. He has launched a new site called Data.gov that is the one place where all information is easy to find, sort, download, and manipulate. He wants to put as much data out there as possible, and then allow the private sector to develop applications for phones or blogs to interpret the data in new and exciting ways. When asked for an example of potential benefits from these efforts, Kundra responded, "There's a lot of data out there—from the National Institutes of Health, the CDC, the FDA—concerning outbreaks and pandemics. There's a lot of Census Bureau data right now. For the first time, the bureau is going to be noting GPS coordinates for addresses across the country. . . . All of a sudden you've got a new layer of information that has never existed before. Imagine if you could build an iPhone app that combined the GPS info with addresses and then combined that with the data about outbreaks."[4]

The availability of global data on sites like Data.gov is increasing daily. Information relating to medicine, education, scientific research, energy, and business is becoming accessible to common individuals. The democratization of data enables comparative analysis of services provided by the government and investments that it makes, leading to a more productive system. When abundant data is out in the open, people gain an even greater voice in public policy decisions. They can be heard through their measurable actions that can now be quantified and interpreted by all.

The proliferation of data will increase productivity throughout all sectors. In the old days, when data was scarce, the actual data was valuable. Now that data is abundant, it's the *utilization* of the data that holds more or less value. Those who can develop software to interpret and deliver abundant data in productive ways will be the biggest winners in the tech revolution. It's the same with energy. New forms of solar, wind, geothermal, and hydrogen energy are becoming accessible to individuals for the first time. Energy is no longer a scarce resource; hence, those who provide the energy will no longer be the ones who reap the greatest profit. The people who create the optimal uses for energy will take home the biggest rewards. The twentieth century was defined by strategies of scarcity. In this century, we will be pursuing the best strategies of abundance.

In the tech revolution everything can be tracked, recorded, and comparatively interpreted. Personal health equipment will track vital signs when you are working out, when you are eating, and while you are sleeping. There will be no more secrets inside the body or outside. The results of your daily activities will be automatically tracked and inserted into comparative databases, thereby revealing a true depiction of yourself. Again, no more secrets.

It can be quite motivational to review a recorded log of your own actions. It becomes easy to identify areas of improvement when the numbers are clearly laid out in front of you. This is already happening with the Nike+ project. With Nike+ my running data is captured instantaneously on my iPod and synched to the Nike Web site, where I can review my start times, duration, and distance. I can browse graphs of my own workouts, I can set goals, and I can compare myself to friends in my running group. I love to see my speed going down a hill and then up a hill, to know exactly at what minute my efficiency declines. This kind of transparency allows runners everywhere to get on a path to better health and better performance. Nike+ has enabled over 1 million people to track their running over 130 million miles and their burning more than 13 billion calories. On August 31, 2008, 779,275 people participated in the Nike organized Human Race. All the runners uploaded their data to Nike+, and together they ran more than 4 million miles across the world. If numeric analysis can happen to this extent in the running world, imagine the possibilities for brain activity, or food intake, or mood monitoring. "What Nike+ taught us about was content," said Trevor Edwards, Nike's vice president of global brand management. "It lets the product live beyond its physical use."

Nike also is trying to tap into the power of communities. Nicholas Christakis, a researcher at Harvard Medical School, has been looking into the behavioral effects of social networking. From one of his focus groups, which included 12,000 people in Framingham, Massachusetts, he found that people tend to quit smoking in groups, as part of a team effort. As more smokers quit, the remaining smokers are more likely to move toward the norm of the social network and try quitting too. We've known for a long time that peer pressure can have a direct effect on people's behavior; it seems that the Web is about to create a new culture of community that allows each of us to gravitate toward those groups we are most interested in. We are no longer held hostage by the physical place we inhabit. If you are fighting cancer, you now can join online cancer social networks. If you love science, you can team up with and exchange ideas with others who are working out difficult questions in online communities.[5]

In this era of abundant information, there will be particularly great rewards for the innovations that make users feel like something more than collected data. Look at Facebook and Twitter. Both platforms allow people to use information to shape and expand the online communities they join. They allow for interaction with experts, celebrities, and friends alike, for thrills or in the pursuit of specific information. Facebook and Twitter members have found that it is easy to keep up to date with family and friends and to hash out the news of the world. Certainly these personal exchanges seem to be far more interesting than news that is broadcast impersonally by strangers. Facebook estimates that every month users share 4 billion pieces of information—news stories, status updates, birthday wishes, and so on. They upload 850 million photos and 8 million videos. If you want to know what a stranger thinks of your favorite movie, you can run a Google search. If you want to know what your friends think, you run a Facebook search. Again, we're just getting started. Data will continue to be made more abundant, relevant, and interconnected through these innovative media platforms in the tech revolution.[6]

Remember J.J. Abrams' conviction that the best stories and shows are character driven? That conviction seems to apply to the Internet as well. Those who dominate the tech revolution will understand that the Internet is ultimately about people, not abundant data. Of course you need the data, but that alone won't ensure your success. Facebook CEO Mark Zuckerberg says, "Nobody wants to live in a surveillance society, which if you take that to its extreme, could be where Google is going." He adds, "It doesn't give people the control that they need to be comfortable."[7] Facebook allows users to control who gains access to their personal data and who doesn't. It's a platform that the general population seems to be more comfortable with.

With all of this in mind, my forecast is that, during Obama's tenure as president, the Nasdaq Technology Index will reclaim its prior highs. Yes, I'm talking about the highs not seen since March 2000, when the index hit 5,000. As I write this, the index sits at 1,800, 64 percent below where it was nine years earlier. So what's behind this optimistic prediction? Look back to the dot-com bubble. Then, many people saw the Internet's vast potential, but after a few years investors lost patience because it proved so difficult to generate real earnings from the Web. Those real earnings have arrived.

I see two reasons why many companies had such a difficult time 10 years ago: first, most had poor business models, and second, the Internet was not universally available at high speeds. Using dial-up Internet was like driving on a muddy, slow, unsafe road in the beginning of the transportation revolution. Combine that with the fact that Microsoft's operating system was slow and regularly infected with viruses and you can see why investors became skeptical. In most households the Internet was more trouble than it was worth. Look around today and you realize how far we've come in a decade. The social structures of family, friends, entertainment, and business can now be navigated on the Web without a hitch. Speaking of getting hitched, a reported 12 percent of newlyweds met online in 2008.[8] This is becoming the new social platform to meet people, to sell products, and to advertise. We are finally on the cusp of the real dot-com run.

Universal access to a high-speed Internet connection through broadband and wireless capabilities will mark the point where the tech revolution starts to realize its growth potential. By 2009 there were approximately 402 million 3G subscribers connected through their mobile phones. That amounts to only 9.8 percent of 4.1 billion mobile phone users worldwide, but the percentage is increasing rapidly. In the countries where 3G was launched first, Japan and South Korea, 3G penetration is over 70 percent. According to a study by ABI Research, $18 billion is being poured into long-term 3G investments that will produce 100 Mbps download speeds to mobile devices by 2014. China recently awarded its first 3G licenses, and it has only just begun implementing the high-speed technology among its 3 billion citizens. 3G is the technology that will truly make this a global event.[9]

This is the dawn of a new era. If you don't believe me, listen to Apple CEO Steve Jobs commenting on the astounding success of his App Store launch, where customers bypassed traditional brick–and-mortar stores and downloaded more than 60 million apps onto their iPhones in the first month of availability: "I've never seen anything like this in my career. . . . Who knows, maybe it will be a $1 billion marketplace at some point in the future." He said this in an interview with the *Wall Street Journal* back in August 2008. Only eight months later, Apple announced that customers had downloaded 1 billion applications from its App Store.

Phil Schiller, Apple's VP of marketing said, "In nine months, the App Store has completely revolutionized the mobile industry, and this is only the beginning."[10]

My forecast that the Nasdaq will reclaim its prior high of 5,000 is based on five potential factors that could catapult the tech revolution into its next phase. If four of the five evolve as I am forecasting, tech investors will be in for some big gains. In short:

- Wireless high-speed Internet access is becoming more and more the standard.
- Alternative energy is changing the way we live.
- Cell-based solutions to health care will reinvigorate innovation into the medical field.
- Cloud computing will improve scientific research and educational pursuits.
- President Obama has a vision for the tech revolution.

Tomorrow the World—In Your Hand

The father of wireless technology was Nikola Tesla, who pioneered this science in the late 1800s and understood it in a way few do even today. "Distance," he said, "which is the chief impediment to human progress, will be completely annihilated in thought, word, and action." Not a bad prognostication? Try this: "One person has to only look into the receiver of an ordinary telephone in one city, and, while talking to a friend a thousand miles away, he can watch the expression of the other's face, criticize the cut of his new suit of clothing, or advise him what to do about that tired look about the eyes." That was a prediction Tesla made in 1899. He further prophesied about the coming revolution when he told Katherine Johnson, "The time will come when crossing the ocean by steamer you will be able to have a daily paper on board with the important news of the world, . . . and by means of a pocket instrument, you can communicate from any distance with friends at home through an instrument similarly attuned." This guy rates with Leonardo da Vinci as a seer. As John Stone said, "Tesla was so far ahead of his time that the best of us then took him for a dreamer."[11]

While it's common to talk about the "worldwide" Internet, in fact most people in the world have yet to connect with it. While over 50 percent of the world's population own a cell phone, only 19 percent of the world's population have access to an Internet link. This phenomenon is known as the "digital divide." Companies like Apple are working to eliminate it by offering inexpensive mobile devices that can surf the Web to its full capacity. Going forward, the most important statistic for investors to track will be mobile Internet market share. Whoever wins this battle will be king of the new world.

With the trend indicating mass migration to the mobile Internet, mobile phone software will differentiate the winners from the losers. Steve Jobs commented on the appeal of iPhone software during a recent conference call: "Competitors are scrambling to copy our App Store, but it's not as easy as it looks, and we are far along in creating the virtuous cycle of cool applications begetting more iPhone sales, thereby creating an even larger market that will attract even more iPhone software development. It is clear that customers are now attracted to iPhone not only for its amazing functionality and revolutionary multitouch user interface but also for its unique ability to let users easily purchase, download, and use thousands of different applications, ranging from free games to financial planning and health management—all of this in only 102 days."[12]

Apple has brought the Internet to the next level. The efficiency of wireless distribution through its online App Store is impossible for the traditional model of distribution to compete with; it spans a host of categories, including gaming, music, video, education, health, business, books, news, social networking, weather, or whatever else you're into. During Q1 of 2009, a quarter in which consumers supposedly quit spending, Apple grew its real revenue by 54.5 percent and grew its net income by a staggering 81.2 percent. That kind of growth is absurd for a company as mature as Apple. That kind of growth is absurd during an economic collapse. But it happened. And it's just the beginning.

On the same conference call, Jobs also said, "I think the traditional game in the phone market has been to produce a voice phone in a hundred different varieties. But as software starts to become the differentiating technology of this product category, I think that people are going to find that a hundred variations presented to a software developer is not very enticing, and most of the competitors in this phone business do not really have much experience in a software platform business. So we are extremely comfortable with our strategy, our product strategy going forward, and we approach it as a software platform company, which is pretty different than most of our competitors."

Apple is no stranger to the importance of software platforms. The Mac operating system (OS), which was fortunate enough to survive the era of Microsoft dominance, provides the Mac computer and the iPhone with a barrier to entry 100 stories high. Even if a new competitor came along and released a superior operating system, it would not be able to penetrate the market. Microsoft did such a good job of building a platform monopoly that it is a miracle the Apple OS even exists. Apple's cultlike following in the 1980s and 1990s kept software developers around during the lean years. Without software, an OS platform is irrelevant. This platform is why the Mac isn't just another computer and why the iPhone isn't just another gadget.

Microsoft's folly with the Vista release has allowed Apple to become a mass market share player. In a 2008 Net Applications Survey, Apple's share of the operating system market grew 5.69 percent to hit a record 7.80 percent, while Windows in all its flavors dropped half a point to 91.17 percent. That's a record low for Microsoft, which nonetheless still runs on 9 out of 10 computers on the Internet. Once a trend like this begins, it is very difficult to reverse it.

Apple is the next Microsoft. But they will be even bigger because they dominate the hardware as well. Legendary investor Warren Buffett says, "In business I look for economic castles protected by unbreachable moats." Thanks to Steve Jobs's reluctance to outsource the Mac OS, Apple is perched in the protected castle. His company will live on much longer than he himself does. Microsoft dominated the last 25 years, and Apple is poised for a similar if not better run. Twenty years ago, this technology was a luxury, but now it has evolved into a worldwide necessity. Apple is ideally positioned to take advantage of the tech revolution.

When you analyze Apple, you'll see that the OS platform is the most important aspect of the company. It insulates the company from short-term competition. By now computers and phones are more than just gadgets; they are essential elements of business and social society. They are necessities that are more important than cars, clothes, and, according to the latest data, even religion. Not a bad era to have the best OS in town.

Mobile devices are only one segment of the wireless generation. While PCs were once the primary means of accessing the Internet, soon everything from your car to your refrigerator will be connected to the global network, communicating with all other things wirelessly. Electrolux, best known for its vacuum cleaners, has developed the ScreenFridge, an Internet refrigerator that manages your pantry, e-mails a shopping list to your local supermarket, and coordinates a convenient delivery time with your schedule. Say hello to a brave, new world.[13]

For decades the television was a one-way device, but once it incorporates 3G Internet access, it will become a two-way affair. Emerging markets will compound the growth potential with innovations that combine the Internet and television in low-cost, natural alternatives with international appeal and the capacity to link with mobile devices.

Ronald Reagan once said, "There are no such things as limits to growth because there are no limits to the human capacity for intelligence, imagination, and wonder." And so it is for this new era of tech. This is a time of growing collective intelligence. We are exploiting unprecedented access to almost all the human knowledge that has ever existed. It blows my mind to think that it's all available with the touch of a screen.

Alternative Today, Standard Tomorrow

I wonder if there are two Charles Mungers in the world. If ever you've attended a Berkshire Hathaway shareholder meeting, you know Charlie Munger as Warren Buffett's longtime, soft-spoken business partner, a man who rarely feeds the media his great investment ideas. It's a different story at a Wesco Financial shareholder meeting. Here, Munger is chairman and freely shares his thoughts and opinions on just about everything. At the 2009 meeting I found two of his takes especially notable. "Ethanol is quite possibly the stupidest thing ever invented by rational people. The ultimate social safety net—which is a very good idea, by the way—is cheap food, and ethanol production is destroying this. It was a monstrously stupid idea like I haven't seen before." And then, "As I move close to the edge of death, I find myself getting more cheerful about the economic future." Munger sees "a final breakthrough that solves the main technical problem of man." By harnessing the power of the sun and wind, he argued, electrical power will become more available around the world. That will help humans turn seawater into freshwater and eliminate environmental problems. "The main technical problem is about to be fixed," he said. "If you have enough energy, you can solve a lot of other problems."

The oil bubble of 2008 reopened everyone's eyes to the importance of developing an alternative energy infrastructure to support the next generation. Barack Obama's alternative energy agenda helped to make him a powerful presidential candidate. Will his agenda be pushed forward even in the face of low oil prices? I think so. There were many industries and companies that were damaged in the recession that are now trying to reestablish a new brand based on green technology. From GM to GE, they are all focused on energy-efficient products. The government is passing legislation to encourage that focus. Who will the winners be? It's hard to predict, but what's certain is that "alternative energy's" transformation into "energy" will benefit the Nasdaq in a major way.

The recent restructuring of the automotive industry was long overdue. America now has an ideal opportunity to reclaim its spot as a leader of automotive innovation. Let's face it, the U.S. auto industry has been run by a bunch of Keystone Kops. GM's model has been broken for 40 years. Conceding the luxury market to Germany put us on a path of pinched margins that we've been stuck on ever since. The dominance of BMW, Mercedes Benz, Porsche, and Volkswagen, not to mention Honda and Toyota, put American companies on shaky ground. The oil bubble brought the final crushing blow. We need a return to quality and innovation; consumers look out for both. Out with the Keystone Kops and in with some new blood.

Ford is an important exception. They took no government bailout money and now find themselves in an environment with fewer GM and Chrysler dealerships to compete against. Ford looks like the company most likely to benefit from the next stage of flex fuel implementation. The company will have a two-year head start over their American counterparts, who will be working on restructuring through bankruptcy, and they will not be subject to any governmental control. Ford LEAPS need to be in your portfolio.

General Electric is shaping up as an alternative energy leader for the next generation. What they're doing in the Middle East with their Masdar City project is like nothing I've ever seen. If you're not familiar with Masdar City, go onto YouTube and check out the latest. It is being constructed 11 miles southeast of Abu Dhabi, the capital of United Arab Emirates. This is a city of the future that utilizes all of the latest green technologies. The city relies entirely on solar energy and other renewable resources such as wind, geothermal, and hydrogen energies, with a zero carbon, zero waste ecology. A solar-powered desalinization plant supplies water needs; water will be recycled as many times as possible and then finished off in crop irrigation. Biological waste will be used to create nutrient-rich soil and fertilizer and recycled for other uses. The city will sustain 50,000 inhabitants and 1,500 businesses specializing in environment-friendly projects. Automobiles are banned within the city; the public and personal transit systems thread through Masdar like something out of the *Jetsons* cartoon.[14]

Living Cells to Replace Pills

On January 23, 2009, the Food and Drug Administration approved the first human trials of embryonic stem cells, which represented a major policy shift between the incoming Obama administration and its predecessor. Geron, a biotech firm, will treat a small group of spinal cord injury patients using neurons derived from stem cells. Upon gaining the approval for the procedure, Geron CEO Thomas Okarma called it "the dawn of a new era in medical therapeutics" in which medicine's purpose will be to "permanently reverse pathology, not merely to temporarily relieve symptoms."[15]

For a long time stem cell innovation within the United States was stalled by deeply rooted religious debates over the role of embryos in scientific research. Now, it will be interesting to see if embryonic stem cells will even be needed; there are great strides being made with adult stem cells and cord blood stem cells. Listening to stem cell professionals explain the potential of this technology leaves me shaking my head in amazement. And it's more than just wishful thinking. Google searches will link you to multiple stories about how stem cells have cured or are close to curing ailments such as blindness, diabetes, heart disease, spinal cord injuries, osteoporosis, liver failure, cystic fibrosis, leukemia, cancer, Parkinson's, and Alzheimer's. Researchers are getting closer and closer to a breakout. The stock market will price in success before it becomes a reality.

A Harvard University scientist, George Church, who is backed by Google and OrbiMed, plans to unlock the secrets of common diseases by decoding the DNA of 100,000 people in the world's biggest gene sequencing project ever. He plans to spend $1 billion to tie DNA information to each person's health history, creating a database from which new medicines can be found. The United States, United Kingdom, China, and Sweden this year began working together to decipher the genetic makeup of 1,000 people, at a cost of $50 million.[16]

Google is looking for ways to give people greater control over their medical data. Along with the unspecified donation to Church, the company is also working with the Cleveland Clinic to better organize health records, and last year Google gave $3.9 million to 23andme Inc., a company that sells genomic data to individuals. The American Recovery Act is also jumping on board: It will support the long-overdue step of computerizing America's medical records to reduce the duplication, waste, and errors that cost billions of dollars and thousands of lives. The Recovery Act has allotted $19.5 billion to this project.

These online records will also unleash the potential for patients to be more active participants in the prevention and treatment of their diseases. A Web-based medical marketplace could open up the globalization of medicine to billions of people. President Obama said, "Because of recent progress—not just in biology, genetics, and medicine but also in physics, chemistry, computer science, and engineering—we have the potential to make enormous progress against diseases in the coming decades. And that's why my administration is committed to increasing funding for the National Institutes of Health, including $6 billion to support cancer research—part of a sustained, multiyear plan to double cancer research in our country." This is all good news for the Nasdaq.[17]

Cloud Computing: Out of the Lab, Out of the Classroom

Cloud computing is the technology of putting software and services on servers "in the cloud" rather than on individual computer hard drives. The growing number of portable, Internet-enabled gadgets that can connect to the Internet will fuel the move toward cloud computing. Consumers can expect to access their crucial data, software, and information wherever they are.

VMware's CEO Paul Maritz had this to say about the future of cloud computing: "We are in a big transition from a device-centric world to an information-centric world. It's going to be about how do you make the information useful and available and make that the center of people's lives instead of specific devices. Devices will have to cleave to the information rather than the other way around. IT infrastructure, the plumbing, will fade away for most users and businesses, and will increasingly be left to professional providers." Internet research firm Gartner predicts that by 2012, 80 percent of Fortune 1000 enterprises will be paying for some cloud computing services, and 30 percent will be paying for cloud computing infrastructure services.[18]

A 2009 press release from Yahoo! Inc. is another signal that cloud computing is well on its way: "Yahoo today announced it has expanded its partnerships with top U.S. universities to advance cloud computing research. The University of California at Berkeley, Cornell University, and the University of Massachusetts at Amherst will join Carnegie Mellon University in using Yahoo!'s cloud computing cluster to conduct large-scale systems software research and explore new applications that analyze Internet-scale data sets, ranging from voting records to online news sources. The cluster has approximately 4,000 processor-cores and 1.5 petabytes of disks." Shankar Sastry, dean of the College of Engineering at the University of California, Berkeley, described the project this way: "Access to the cluster is a first step in helping us analyze the vast amounts of societal-scale information available on the Web, such as voting records, online news sources, and polling data. The Yahoo! cluster will also enable us to conduct computationally intensive econometrics research, combining economic theory with statistics to analyze and test large-scale economic relationships." Bob Constable, dean of the faculty of Computing and Information Science at Cornell University, added: "Our partnership with Yahoo! will enable us to attack problems ranging from wildlife preservation and biodiversity, to balancing socioeconomic needs and the environment, to large-scale deployment and management of renewable energy sources."[19]

A President Focused on Technology

President Obama's Recovery Act stimulus package provides $7.2 billion for increasing high-speed broadband Internet access nationwide. The package includes grants for deploying broadband access in rural areas, expanding computer center capacity, and encouraging sustainable broadband adoption initiatives. The president believes that modernized infrastructure is a necessary part of the foundation needed to achieve long-term economic stability and prosperity. That infrastructure includes everything from a comprehensive national broadband plan, to new health care information technology, to a modernized electricity grid. The stimulus package provides more than $34 billion for a smart electricity grid, $4.5 billion for greening office buildings, and, as I mentioned previously, $20 billion for digitizing health care records. What oil was to President Bush, clean energy and technology is to President Obama.

An IBM research report concluded that $30 billion spent in 2009 on the smart grid, broadband access, and digitized health care records would create approximately 949,000 jobs. The total package will end up costing more than the entire Iraq War.

To finish this chapter, and tie up the argument for a bullish Nasdaq in the future, I'm going to defer to our forty-fourth chief executive, who is much more eloquent than I. The following are excerpts from a speech President Obama gave at the National Academy of Sciences on April 27, 2009, and they clearly present the vision behind his tech agenda:

Today, of course, we face more complex challenges than we have ever faced before: a medical system that holds the promise of unlocking new cures and treatments—attached to a health care system that holds the potential for bankruptcy to families and businesses; a system of energy that powers our economy, but simultaneously endangers our planet; threats to our security that seek to exploit the very interconnectedness and openness so essential to our prosperity; and challenges in a global marketplace which links the derivative trader on Wall Street to the homeowner on Main Street, the office worker in America to the factory worker in China—a marketplace in which we all share in opportunity, but also in crisis. At such a difficult moment, there are those who say we cannot afford to invest in science, that support for research is somehow a luxury at moments defined by necessities. I fundamentally disagree. Science is more essential for our prosperity, our security, our health, our environment, and our quality of life than it has ever been before.

Federal funding in the physical sciences as a portion of our gross domestic product has fallen by nearly half over the past quarter century. . . . We have watched as scientific integrity has been undermined and scientific research politicized in an effort to advance predetermined ideological agendas. We know that our country is better than this. I believe it is not in our character, the American character, to follow. It's our character to lead. And it is time for us to lead once again. So I'm here today to set this goal: We will devote more than 3 percent of our GDP to research and development. We will not just meet, but we will exceed the level achieved at the height of the space race, through policies that invest in basic and applied research, create new incentives for private innovation, promote breakthroughs in energy and medicine, and improve education in math and science. This represents the largest commitment to scientific research and innovation in American history. Just think what this will allow us to accomplish: solar cells as cheap as paint; green buildings that produce all the energy they consume; learning software as effective as a personal tutor; prosthetics so advanced that you could play the piano again; an expansion of the frontiers of human knowledge about ourselves and the world around us. . . . The commitment I am making today will fuel our success for another 50 years. That's how we will ensure that our children and their children will look back on this generation's work as that which defined the progress and delivered the prosperity of the twenty-first century.

When the Soviet Union launched Sputnik a little more than a half century ago, Americans were stunned. The Russians had beaten us to space. And we had to make a choice: We could accept defeat or we could accept the challenge. And as always, we chose to accept the challenge. President Eisenhower signed legislation to create NASA and to invest in science and math education, from grade school to graduate school. And just a few years later, a month after his address to the 1961 Annual Meeting of the National Academy of Sciences, President Kennedy boldly declared before a joint session of Congress that the United States would send a man to the moon and return him safely to the Earth. The scientific community rallied behind this goal and set about achieving it. And it would not only lead to those first steps on the moon; it would lead to giant leaps in our understanding here at home. That Apollo program produced technologies that have improved kidney dialysis and water purification systems; sensors to test for hazardous gases; energy-saving building materials; fire-resistant fabrics used by firefighters and soldiers. More broadly, the enormous investment in that era—in science and technology, in education and research funding—produced a great outpouring of curiosity and creativity, the benefits of which have been incalculable. There are those of you in this audience who became scientists because of that commitment. We have to replicate that.

Yes, scientific innovation offers us a chance to achieve prosperity. It has offered us benefits that have improved our health and our lives—improvements we take too easily for granted. But it gives us something more. At root, science forces us to reckon with the truth as best as we can ascertain it. And some truths fill us with awe. Others force us to question long-held views. Science can't answer every question, and indeed, it seems at times the more we plumb the mysteries of the physical world, the more humble we must be. Science cannot supplant our ethics or our values, our principles or our faith. But science can inform those things and help put those values—these moral sentiments, that faith—can put those things to work—to feed a child, or to heal the sick, to be good stewards of this Earth. We are reminded that with each new discovery and the new power it brings comes new responsibility; that the fragility, the sheer specialness of life requires us to move past our differences and to address our common problems, to endure and continue humanity's strivings for a better world. As President Kennedy said when he addressed the National Academy of Sciences more than 45 years ago: "The challenge, in short, may be our salvation."[20]

ten

CASE STUDY: CHINA'S OBSESSION WITH THE YEAR 2020

I n A *Tale of Two Cities*, Charles Dickens depicted the brutal oppression of the French proletariat by aristocratic overlords and then, during and after the famous revolution, a reversal of the brutality as the revolutionaries brought the guillotine down on their former masters. It's a circumstance that has been sadly common in our world's history. In every oppressed population, there is a yearning for vengeance upon those who exploit their labor.

China is a modern-day tale of two cities, but this is a tale still being told. So far, the Chinese government miraculously has managed to introduce bits and pieces of free market capitalism to portions of society without provoking those who get left behind. China in many ways is an anomaly, a case study for an incremental, measured injection of open democratic markets into a long-standing Communist framework. History is being written right before our very eyes as the Chinese government tries to keep control of a process that affects its hundreds of millions of citizens directly and the rest of the world by association.

So far, the ruling political class has managed to avoid the fate of the French autocrats that Dickens so memorably dramatized. How have they done it? Will this experiment blow up in their faces?

I have my own ideas regarding China's peaceful ascent up the global economic ladder, and this information should give you a rare perspective when considering whether or not to invest in Chinese LEAPS. Once you absorb the details of my China theory, you'll start to see supporting evidence everywhere.

The Chinese secret to a peaceful economic ascent is built upon the allure of the year 2020. The Chinese government is obsessed with 2020, the upper class is working toward massive 2020 innovations, and the lower class believes it will achieve true freedom by 2020. The 2020 plan has created an unprecedented, complementary existence between the upper and lower classes that has expanded this empire at a rate never before seen in the history of humankind. If the rest of the world enables China's plan or at least believes in the rhetoric, China will obtain global economic and military dominance without even a hiccup. China's success depends on the free world's accepting and profiting from a labor system that depends on conditions that are effectively slavery. As long as this cheap labor continues to produce an enormous share of the world's goods, China's economic influence will continue to grow throughout the world.

The Propaganda Machine

It all starts with the Communist propaganda machine. You saw it in full effect during the opening ceremonies of the 2008 Summer Olympic Games when the adorable nine-year-old girl Lin Miaoke sang "Ode to the Motherland" while the Chinese national flag entered the Bird's Nest Stadium in Beijing. Her beautiful voice was meant to inspire the world audience and celebrate China's progress. Only it wasn't hers. The voice, that is. What we all heard was actually a recording of another child, Yang Peiyi, whose physical features apparently didn't convey the precise image, internal feelings, and expression that Chinese authorities wanted to show to the world. This was an opportunity for all of us to understand that what China chooses to show us cannot be trusted as truth. For every spotlighted architectural marvel in Beijing or Shanghai, there are thousands of laborers being exploited in that city's outskirts. As long as the world is content to follow the tracks of the spotlights, as the leadership intends, China will continue to appear to thrive.[1]

Nicholas Cull, director of the USC Masters of Public Diplomacy Program, participated in the United States–China Economic Review Commission hearings, where he covered topics that should be important to all investors. He is one of the few who are willing to speak up about the truth behind the Chinese propaganda. "There are three basic points of origin for contemporary Chinese Public Diplomacy," he said. "First is a traditional Chinese concern with issues of image in all relationships. Second is the history of external propaganda practiced by the Communist regime. Third is the recent realization of the central role that Public Diplomacy and communication must take in the new world. The regime carefully selected those aspects of China that would be seen abroad, and censored much of the rest. Favored journalists were allowed glimpses of the nation, while state journals like *Beijing Review* showcased achievements. Radio Beijing harangued the world about the Chairman's monopoly on virtue. The regime sought to export its revolution by sponsoring Communist Parties in East Asia and later in Africa and Latin America."[2]

In February 1999, President Jiang Zemin called for China to "establish a publicity capacity to exert an influence on world opinion that is as strong as China's international standing." In 2007, President Hu Jintao formally called for the Seventeenth National Congress of the Communist Party to enhance the "soft power" of Chinese culture through methods that included management of the Internet and investment in cultural institutions at home. "The great rejuvenation of the Chinese nation," he argued, "will definitely be accomplished by the thriving of Chinese culture."[3]

According to Cull, the central message of Chinese Public Diplomacy is that the country is back as a world power after a 200-year hiatus, that Chinese culture is admirable, and that China's intentions are benign. This last is conveyed through the expression "peaceful rise" and, from 2007, an expressed intent to "build a harmonious world." The message comes directly from President Hu Jintao and flows outward along the party ideological apparatus. In an age of accelerated and expanding informational networks, every country that has advanced has effectively disseminated powerful propaganda about its cultural ideals and value concepts among its population and has also exported those values to the outside world. Internet-enhanced cultural propaganda capabilities are already essential elements in a national culture's soft strength.

China realizes that being a global citizen and trade partner will allow it to maximize the unfair advantage created by its slave labor system. But it also relies on other nations for support and acceptance. China's leaders know their system isn't perfect, and that's why they go to such great lengths to sell an idealized version of themselves through propaganda.

Once a Communist, Always a Communist

Communists are committed to perpetuating their own power. They look for ways to increase it, not the opposite. Whenever you encounter democracy-praising rhetoric of Chinese leaders, just reread the history of 1989 Tiananmen Square massacre. It started off as a peaceful protest by students who were mourning the death of a pro-free market, prodemocracy official, Hu Yaobang. The movement lasted seven weeks before tanks came in on June 4 and left many civilians dead or severely injured. Nobody knows how many people died because the Chinese government won't release those figures, but even its own reports admit that 7,000 were wounded. Immediately thereafter the Communist government banned the foreign press from the country, strictly controlled coverage in its own press, and purged from its government high-ranking officials who had sympathized with the protestors. Many estimate that thousands were brutally murdered. If China was willing to massacre unarmed students engaged in peaceful, prodemocracy meetings in Tiananmen Square back in 1989, how receptive to an open, tolerant society can they be today? Remember that communism and democracy are philosophies with fundamental differences; each is so utterly offended by the other that they cannot coexist.[4]

In the aftermath of the Tiananmen crackdown, Beijing engaged the international public relations firm Hill and Knowlton to rebuild China's image abroad. Simultaneously, domestic and international information networks were consolidated under the umbrella State Council Information Office (SCIO), founded in 1991. The SCIO's declared purpose was to "promote China as a stable country in the process of reform, a China that takes good care of its population, including minorities, and works hard to reduce poverty." It was a foundation for future work.[5]

China's Economic Evolution

China's transformation from a walled-off, centrally planned economy to a modern amalgam of economic principles began in 1978, when a massive drought caused government officials to ease their tight controls over individual farmers' plots. Under new laws, the farmers were allowed to keep their produce either for consumption or sale. The slow march toward a market-based economy has been in progress ever since. The agricultural growth that followed the drought surpassed all expectations, which encouraged further deregulation and the development of farm markets. Little by little this pattern spread to other sectors of the economy and to a gradual liberalization of prices, a new banking system, the development of stock markets, and the opening to foreign trade and investment in the new nonstate sector of business.

By the late 1990s most state enterprises had been sold to private interests, and banks had been transformed to operate increasingly as businesses. Government budgets morphed from being parts of a system of slush-fund cubbyholes into being parts of a modern tax revenue system, with expenditure discipline, based on a single-treasury account. The population migrated in droves to urban areas. The result has been that an education now brings premium pay in virtually all jobs, and public education up through nine grades is now universal. Limited-access highways crisscross every province, and a telecommunications and Internet backbone stretches to country towns and beyond. Among the various underpinnings of China's growth performance, it is difficult to overemphasize the importance of public investment. Typical examples are good roads and highways, ports, airports, high-throughput telecommunications networks, education, public health, law and order, mass transportation, and water and sewage treatment facilities. A wide variety of other structures and facilities provide much needed physical space for profit-oriented enterprises and individuals.

One means for China to concentrate its many resources in public investments so effectively is its two-pronged financial system. The first prong is a well-run directed-credit system that channels funds from bank and postal deposits to policy-determined public uses. The second is a profit-oriented and competitive system, albeit in early and inefficient stages of development. Both prongs continue to undergo rapid government-sponsored reforms. All of these shifts and developments in China's domestic circumstances have not only generated growth in their own right but have also enabled the nation to capitalize on the increasingly open commercial practices and more advanced technologies available from global markets. China can grow so fast because it is so easy to see what the long-term economic goals are and because it is so easy to purchase and otherwise acquire the means to pursue those goals. This "catch-up" growth involves more than factory technologies and modern machinery for ensuring output quality. Like Japan in the nineteenth century, China is studying and importing management and regulatory systems, innovation techniques, and other institutional solutions to its public and for-profit governance challenges.[6]

By the year 2000 output had quadrupled. According to CIA data, as of January 2009 China's population totaled 1.3 billion, with 43 percent of the population urbanized and contributing to the economic growth that now places China as the second largest economy in the world in terms of purchasing power parity. However, on a per capita basis, the Chinese economy lags significantly behind other global leaders.

Private enterprise has grown to encompass 30 million private businesses that account for approximately 70 percent of China's national output, up from 1 percent in 1978. The stock market in Shanghai has doubled in size since 2005. Since economic liberalization began in 1978, the investment- and export-led economy has grown 70 times bigger. Its foreign exchange reserves have reached $1.9 trillion, the largest in the world. China's dollar holdings give the country considerable financial leverage in the world economy. In 2007 and 2008, China's sovereign wealth funds (SWFs) provided much-needed capital to weakened Wall Street financial and brokerage firms.[7]

China's military spending has increased threefold in the past decade according to estimates by the Stockholm International Peace Research Institute. In 2006, it surpassed Japan as the largest military spender in East Asia, and China now has the third largest military budget in the world. China has been upgrading its naval capabilities, improving its ballistic missile arsenals, and entering high-tech arenas, including the militarization of space.

In another break with the twentieth century, there is a convergence of interests between China and Russia. In 2006, China became the number 1 economic partner of Russia, and China has also been financing important Russian pipeline projects. Both

China and Russia are providing arms to oil and gas producers in the third world. Both are increasing their military capability in key energy producing regions. And both powers joined together in 2001 to form the Shanghai Cooperation Organization (SCO) of Central Asian countries.[8]

Joining the United States as a Global Leader

Every so often the world experiences some game changing shifts of power. The catalyst for China's joining the global elite was the country's decision to adopt new policies that distanced China from the stifling socialist and communist regimes of the past. With the new system coming into place, the Chinese people have gained access to the world's free market economy and capitalist system. As the country has become more acquainted with the affluence of the West, the 1.3 billion inhabitants of China are seeking a better quality of life. They are driven by the same motivations and spirit that American pioneers displayed in the nineteenth century.

Where is all of this headed? As long as the world allows China to engage in globalization, it will continue its aggressive growth. This growth will enable China to continue buying up debt in the United States and other countries. Economic success will further legitimize China's form of governance. Strategic partnerships will make ever more countries dependent upon China's money. By keeping its good face spotlighted in all endeavors, China is and will be able to keep global partners in business with them.

And so, the global partners aren't supposed to see or care about the inhumane labor conditions that are still widespread. After all,

all that cheap labor generates trillions of dollars in revenue and greater global influence. China is doing its best to change the world's perception and definition of who it is. If China is seen as a benign and progressive society, no one will perceive a possible Chinese threat or danger to the free West. Meanwhile China can continue to step up its growth, militarily as well as economically, and evolve into a superpower.

As long as acceptance of China remains the status quo, as an investor I'll agree with U.K. Foreign Secretary David Miliband, who describes China as the twenty-first century's indispensable power. China is slowly but surely emerging as a global force alongside the United States in a trend that appears to be a legitimate long-term reality. China's defining moment occurred at the 2008 summer Olympics, where it showcased its economic growth to the rest of the world. China was the only major power to elude the recession of 2007 to 2009—in fact, it overcame the global headwinds to realize a growth rate of 8 percent.

As most nations, including the United States, struggled to implement solutions to the banking crisis and consumer spending slowdown, China attacked its problems quickly and decisively. It implemented an economic stimulus package equivalent to 16 percent of its GDP over two years. "Historians will look back at 2009 and see that China played an incredibly important role in stabilizing global capitalism. That is very significant and sort of ironic," Miliband said in an interview with the *Guardian*. "There's a joke that goes: after 1989, capitalism saved China. After 2009, China saved capitalism."[9]

In Peter Schiff's book *Bull Moves in Bear Markets*, he compares the current state of China to the United States in the 1950s. Back then, our consumer spending was strong, manufacturing was thriving, and economic growth was at an all time high. The U.S. Treasury held more the 60 percent of the world's foreign currency reserves. The dollar was backed by gold and was in strong demand. Fast-forward to the present and you find that the United States has turned into a service-based economy with our manufacturing sector at a competitive disadvantage to producers in Asia who are less burdened by regulation, high taxes, and mandated worker benefits. America has become a nation of consumers while China has become a nation of producers. The implications are interesting: in the United States, the balance of trade is being run at a huge deficit, with imports exceeding exports by $800 billion annually. The federal budget deficit ranges between $300 billion and $400 billion per year, caused by trillions of dollars of government spending for wars, entitlement programs, and debt services. The U.S. national debt is well over $9 trillion, and much of it is owned by China. Underfunded liabilities such as Social Security, veterans' benefits, and loan guarantees raise total government obligations to over $50 trillion. Remember that 50 years ago this nation held 60 percent of the world's reserve currency? Today, foreign currency reserves held by the United States total a mere 1 percent of reserves, putting us behind Libya, Poland, and Turkey. Peter Schiff's research paints quite a sobering picture.[10]

The Chinese Cultural Dynamic

As far as Chinese city culture is concerned, the standard of living is rapidly catching up to the Western world. Transportation has improved significantly since the late 1990s, thanks to a government effort to link the entire nation through a series of expressways. Private car ownership is increasing at an annual rate of 15 percent. Millions of people have tasted the benefits of capitalism for the first time.

National Geographic dedicated its entire May 2008 publication to China and called the issue *Inside the Dragon*. It offered an inside look at the good, the bad, and the ugly of this rising power. Some random but interesting statistics listed in that edition:

- 72 percent of all U.S. shoes are made in China
- 80 percent of U.S. toys are made in China
- six is the number of months that it would take a Chinese factory worker to earn the cost of one Thomas the Tank Engine set
- 96 percent of Chinese car owners pay for their vehicles in cash
- 119 baby boys are born for every 100 girls because of abortion
- the number of unmarried young men is predicted to be 30 million by 2020
- 350 million Chinese smoke an average of 20 cigarettes a day
- 41.5 percent claim that they are nonreligious. A strong sense of nationalism motivates these people. China is all they know. They seem to have grown up with an unquestioning devotion to country and are willing to do whatever it takes to advance the cause.[11]

I think we now have a clear view of what has happened in rural China over the last 30 years, and you have to admit that it is a great thing to see so many millions of people savoring the improvements that a little freedom brings. Property rights. Private business. Investment. Competition. Every step that China takes in this direction will continue to produce growth, and investors would be wise to own some Chinese holdings on this thesis.

But we can't forget about the lack of freedom that rules the unseen majority of China. These are the people who weren't allowed to show up at the Olympics. They're the ones the media aren't allowed to talk about. In spite of all the progress, there are still almost 800 million Chinese living in severe hardship, more than twice the total population of the United States. Cost-minimizing, high-profit, rapid growth is a key objective of China's ruling class. It is based on the exploitation of wage labor and peasant labor. A typical factory worker might earn $1 a day for working 18 hours. He has no choices. He can't choose where to live. He can't choose an occupation. He is a slave to the state that supplies the globe with its inexpensive necessities.

The Sichuan earthquake in the spring of 2008 took a toll among China's poor: badly built schools collapsed and many children died. China's government claims that it provides ideal leadership and that it wants to meet the people's needs, but it does a terrible job in the slum areas. Peasants still have to pay fees for medical services and schooling.[12]

It is not unusual for low-paid wage laborers in the export sector to work 80-hour weeks in factories with abominable health and safety conditions. In the West, we hear about the lead paint in toys produced in China, but not about the toxic fumes being inhaled, the injuries suffered, and limbs lost by the workers in those toy factories. According to one Chinese government survey, 72 percent of the country's nearly 100 million migrant workers are owed unpaid wages. Significantly, China's economic boom of 1990 to 2002 actually led to a decline in formal wage employment in the urban sector, as the state sector sought to achieve greater efficiency and profitability.

Of the 10 most polluted cities in the world, 5 are in China. The Three Gorges Dam project, the scale of which is unparalleled in human history, has wreaked massive destruction on ecosystems and uprooted huge populations. Ravenous commercial development is destroying farmland at a quickening pace (farmers are pressured by local government officials to sell their land-use rights and are barely compensated for doing so). China has now lost half of its wetlands. Capitalist development is an ecological disaster. It has been estimated that air pollution, water pollution, and other forms of environmental degradation are responsible for disease and premature deaths claiming the lives of some 400,000 people in China each year.[13]

The Allure of 2020

So how does the Chinese government keep this 1.3 billion people machine running? It has instilled a message of hope in its own people and sent out a message of tolerance to the world. Remember how we talked about the lack of judgment in society back in the investment log chapter? Well, this era of no judgments is playing to China's advantage. Nobody in the modern world is willing to confront China on human rights issues; instead, we listen to its propaganda and believe it.

Chinese President Hu Jintao loves to talk about the year 2020. His most common international talking point is that by 2020, China's GDP will reach $4 trillion with a per capita GDP of $3,000. China plans to achieve this by further developing the economy, expanding democracy, advancing science and education, improving social justice, improving the people's well–being, and fostering greater social harmony. He understands that the superpower China cannot grow in isolation, which explains the country's aggressive outreach and pursuit of strategic alliances and trade partners.[14]

By focusing on the year 2020, Hu buys himself some valuable time among the labor class of China. Hu's projections for the year 2020 have been included in speeches given in April 2004, May 2005, November 2005, June 2006, May 2007, October 2007, December 2007, November 2008, and April 2009. He has claimed that he is committed to seizing this moment of opportunity to build a prosperous society. In a 2006 visit to Yale University, he referenced 2020 by announcing that by then, the political landscape will have improved greatly. Anything before then is just too soon.[15]

Do you really believe this guy? Do you think he really wants to give *that much* power to the people? In China, the goal of $3,000 per capita GDP by 2020 represents the threshold for democracy. This is the level of affluence, it is believed, at which people will be positioned to demand their rights and protect their property. It sounds to me as though Hu has bought himself at least 10 years of willing, cheap labor to help grow the empire. But what dividend will he be willing to pay to the majority of his citizens?

Members of China's leadership have forecasted that the Chinese Peoples Liberation Army by 2020 will have achieved an overall modernization of its logistic sector, and it will be able to fight and win wars in the information age.[16] China intends to launch its own space station in 2020, according to one of the country's leading space experts.[17] Another goal is to establish a health care network that, by 2020, will cover every man, woman, and child in China.[18]

China's 2020 vision extends to just about every aspect of society. In the run-up to the G-20 summit, China's top policymakers were shrill about the need for developing an alternative to the U.S. dollar as a global reserve currency by 2020. They have also talked up their plan to double reliance on renewable energy by 2020. These are awfully rosy projections, all set to hit in the same year. What a coincidence.

President Hu spelled out the details of the 2020 plan for his people by breaking down the cooperative requirements into four aspects (it's long so I'll include just the highlights):

1. Development should be given top priority, as it is key to meeting challenges on the way toward modernization. Only development can help to support the Chinese people's standard of living, ensure that China takes its due responsibility in international affairs, and make it possible for the country to contribute more to the development of the world economy.

2. The people always come first. Serving the people is the fundamental purpose of the Party. There will be prosperity for all, and development is for the people, by the people, and with the people.

3. China must pursue comprehensive, balanced, and sustainable development that is in accord with the overall arrangement of socialism with Chinese characteristics.

4. There must be persistence in the overall consideration of the current social situation. The major relationships in the cause of socialism with Chinese characteristics must be correctly understood and managed. Urban and rural development must be balanced, and there must be development among regions as well as economic and social development, relations between human beings and nature must be managed, and there must be domestic development and openings to the outside world.[19]

Did you get the message? I'll forever pair the words "development" with the phrase "socialism with Chinese characteristics." I'm surprised he didn't remind the people about the need for "peaceful progress" as he has done in every other speech he's ever given. Of course he wants peace. He's the dictator! A revolution would take him out. He's doing what needs to be done to the 800 million people who are forced to live like animals while the Communist leadership, sorry, the socialists with Chinese characteristics, use them to build up their 2020 empire. I will be very shocked if widespread freedom is given to the Chinese people as promised.

But however troubling the plight of those masses may be, the numbers indicate that China is going to own the world by 2020. As long as the Chinese people and the rest of the world buy into the rhetoric, it will become a self-fulfilling prophecy: 2020 will be the year of China.

President Hu's call for a "harmonious world" is in China's best interest because China knows where it stands in such a world. China wins. Its working class gives the Chinese a strategic advantage in a world in which other developed nations are forced to play by the modern rules governing human rights. As China continues to oppress so many of its own people, Hu lays out three basic principles (very convenient) of a "harmonious world":

- We need to uphold the spirit of inclusiveness and acknowledge the differences in civilization and culture as basic features of humanity that have played an important role in human progress.
- We will foster mutual respect by treating each other as equals and respecting the right of a nation to choose its social system and development mode. Harmonious but different.
- We need multilateralism to ensure common security and enable democratized international relations.[20]

President Obama appears to share this vision. His appointees in foreign affairs will be tasked with cleaning up the divisive, international mess that George W. Bush created. As long as President Hu and President Obama play well together, Chinese prosperity will surge. China will keep producing, and the rest of the world will keep buying and sustain strong diplomatic ties. If the United States decides to stand up for human rights in China it will spell the end of Chinese growth, and I will buy as many Chinese LEAPS puts as I can get my hands on.

But if China continues to exploit its cheap, inhumane labor advantage and achieves dominance, with that power will come arrogance. Its morals are compromised because it is willing to do to its workers what others will not; and the more powerful it becomes, the less it will feel a need to address those morals. This is not an even playing field. It's like competing with an athlete who is on steroids. Since no living Americans have experienced anything like the exploitation of the Chinese proletariat (unless they've come here from an oppressive state), we fail to understand the dynamics. The Chinese ruling class is going global in pursuit of its own interests, not in pursuit of freedom and openness at home. The improvement in economic conditions is not linked to the goal of a democratic society. Historically Communists are always committed to the concentration and expansion of their own power.

But you can bet that the Chinese won't be saying so on trade missions or in speeches meant for the rest of the world to hear. Then it will be all about "harmony" and "respect for those who choose a different government," and that's the message China will stick to until it has achieved its superpower status. And what happens then? What happens when China begins to flex its new muscles? What happens after their unfair wealth advantage has helped it secure majority ownership in companies and governments in the West?

As an investor, am I worried about inflation coming from China? No. This was and remains a Communist state, and it will continue to exploit its lower-class workers as long as it benefits those in power to do so. Higher-priced items coming out of China will only be a rumor. But who will win big as long as there is no definitive characterization of the Chinese political and economic system?

So many in the West simply do not know what to make of this nation. On one hand, it's allowing many of its citizens to acquire wealth and it is embracing a market-based economy, and on the local level it actually has "democratic parties" running candidates in open village and town elections. On the other, it's the same old Communist Party of China running the show and doing nothing for 800 million workers who are treated like slaves. Heavy restrictions remain on the Internet, the press, freedom of assembly, reproductive rights, and religious practice. It's a contradiction with 1.3 billion people, and the world's deck is stacked in its favor. More and more it seems that China will become exactly what it chooses to be.

Investors need to be aware of these developments because it is inevitable by now that what happens in China affects the fortunes of the United States. An alpha investor must accept that a global China will be a nation of perhaps unprecedented growth. This growth will enable China to continue buying up debt of the United States and other countries, which in turn buys its government and its practices legitimacy. Strategic partnerships likely will continue to make ever more countries reliant on China's money.

As an investor, you should make a good play in this action. As an American, you might be more than a little worried about the implications.

conclusion

HARNESSING
THE ELEMENTS

M ost investors need metaphors to define their strategies. Many are comfortable with references to betting and horse racing. By now you've seen that I'm inspired by sports and historical legends, with a few lessons from flying, weather, and other technological achievements thrown into the mix. As you find your own way as an investor, you'll find the words, stories, and concepts that work for you; in the meantime, do your best to deconstruct the analogies used by people who have ridden out these volatile times (so far).

At some time in prerecorded history it's likely the world experienced a cataclysmic event that resulted in many floods and rising seas and rivers. The ancient literature of most cultures includes either an account of recovering after the waters rose or the legend of a single man who rode above the waves to preserve humanity. The Book of Genesis gives us the story of Noah's ark; the Greeks wrote of Deucalion, who survived the deluge unleashed by Zeus;

the Hindus have the story of Manu. The Shujing from China, among the earliest known historical texts, describes the irrigation systems that were built to utilize the floodwater that covered the majority of Asia. To develop effective agricultural techniques, Jews, Christians, and Muslims of Mesopotamia worked diligently to understand weather patterns. The archeological record shows the modern world that from the beginning, harnessing the elements was a requirement for establishing an enduring civilization. This, again, is alpha.

It seems that one of the early practitioners of alpha was a man named Enoch, who has made his way into accounts as varied as the Dead Sea Scrolls, the Zohar text of Kabbalah, and the New Testament (where he is quoted at least 128 times). He was a resident of Sumer, one of the first cities to flourish in Mesopotamia. Apparently he had a very unusual and sophisticated relationship with his environment, and he understood when his civilization had moved out of accord with the laws of nature. It was a time of great upheaval: the skies darkened, torrential rains were followed by terrible droughts, there were meteoric disturbances, and the seas pulled back from the land. And all these were just preliminary disturbances; the great flood was still to come. The historian Hugh Nibley describes Enoch as the great observer and recorder of all things in heaven and earth, as a seer who conveyed to men the mind and will of God. Because he was so perfectly in tune with the happenings of the day, he could exercise control of the elements. When he spoke, the mountains shook and rivers turned their courses.[1]

Just like Enoch, it is important for us as investors to think for ourselves and not be victimized by the conditions we face. We must learn to survive the new volatility that has entered the global economy. The commotion of markets that is exacerbated by the four winds of Wall Street—online trading, hedge funds, bubbles, and unintended consequences of government intervention—must be accepted, understood, and exploited. Cycles are a part of every human life.

Many who shun investing themselves look at us investors and think we're gambling our money away in the stock market. They also don't think that the stock market has any effect on their nine-to-five jobs and comfortable lives. But everyone is affected by what happens in the markets. Globalization means that all people are slowly being drawn into one unified conglomerate, whether we like it or not. Self-sufficiency will soon be an ideal of the past.

Whether this reliance on technology and specialization of labor is a blessing or a curse I don't know, but I accept that it is a force in the world and that we should all be vigilant observers of economic conditions so that we can protect our wealth, which in turn provides for our families.

In the introduction of this book, I outlined my nine exemplary investment traits as they were embodied in nine exceptional individuals. Each trait will play a role in the investor's success on the new Wall Street.

John F. Kennedy provided me with the inspiration to dig deeper into the effects of globalization. From there, I was able to recognize China as *the* global player that must be watched vigilantly. If we get this one wrong, our portfolios will suffer. JFK also had the ability to stand against the crowd, a trait that allows us to anticipate the bursting of a speculative bubble when the momentum players are trying to persuade us that there is a new status quo.

Steve Jobs is a perfect example of why economic timing can be such a valuable indicator for investment decisions. Jobs is a seer who identifies the direction that society is heading, and he makes decisions based on that knowledge. It's difficult to make any micro-portfolio decisions about which stocks to buy or sell without a sure knowledge of the macroeconomic trends. Economic timing provides us with numeric clarity as we determine where we're at in each investment cycle. You can't be too far ahead, but you need to be far *enough* ahead to take part in the stock price action. Economic timing is a commonsense model that takes into account the most important economic variables like GDP, employment, inflation, and consumer confidence, and it calculates the rate of change of each.

If Steve Jobs represents the macrostrategy, then J.J. Abrams homes in on the microstrategy. His example guides us in the selection of individual companies. We want to own option LEAPS calls on companies with positive uncertainty in a growing economy, and we want to own LEAPS puts on companies with negative uncertainty in a worsening economy. To figure out which companies to own, look no further than the specific products of each. Growth is derived from great products.

The famous Frost-Nixon interview frames a key lesson for crisis investing. As we struggle with investment decisions during a crisis, it is important to ask the right questions so that we can identify the root cause, those who are affected by the root cause, and the solutions that will work and those that will not. A failure to ask the right questions will put you at the mercy of the media and politicians who are seeking to deflect blame away from their interests and allies. Beginning each market morning with a question of the day is a great way to keep you in tune with the market-moving variables.

John Wooden did things the right way. He was not concerned with winning as much as he was with executing his practices at a high level. He knew that the winning would take care of itself. As an investor, I can't control the daily swings in the market, but I can control my strategic process and, hopefully, realize high returns over the long run. As long as I am thorough and efficient with my research, I'm confident that the profits will take care of themselves. Whenever I follow one of my investment rules, I think of John Wooden. It's all about smart execution.

Because it is impossible to predict the daily moves of the market, there always will be short-term setbacks to overcome. George Washington's resilience is the perfect example to follow every step of the way. When the detailed process of Economic LEAPS investing feels overwhelming, think back to General Washington's defying the odds by refusing to accept defeat. In the end, the rewards were worth the sacrifice.

Tommy Lasorda's decision to turn to his superstar, Kirk Gibson, when he needed him illustrates why I use option LEAPS. LEAPS are more gifted than stocks. Their inherent ability to maximize gains through a system of economic timing makes investing worth all the time and effort. You're not going to outperform the market unless your superstars are in the game. Sometimes you can use them only to pinch hit, but they need to be on the roster to do you any good.

Societal trends are manifested through the symbology of stocks. Study of the symbols guided my research and conclusions regarding the tech revolution. There's no symbol more important than high-speed wireless connection: once it is available to the masses, it will break down barriers of communication in ways and to an extent that we haven't seen since the transportation revolution. Find the symbols that represent governmental, cultural, and technological developments.

Finally, put it all together to achieve alpha. The band Keane showed me what can happen when each member of a group maximizes the potential of his or her individual talents. The resulting sound was dazzling. Such is the goal of alpha investors. I put all of the moving pieces of the market together by writing in my investment log. The log is where the reams of information available on the Internet can be sorted into relevant segments of research; it's in the log that I can put the critical information together in an order that helps me to purchase the right LEAPS at the right time.

Once you've captured the perfect LEAPS by synthesizing these traits and practices, you'll have it: the exhilaration of alpha.

We need to prepare for the future of investing without fear. We're living in exciting times—don't expect the coming years to be boring—and we need a proactive approach to investment management to win in the up cycles and survive the down cycles. I hope that this book has opened your eyes to some of the structural changes that have influenced the stock market, and I hope it's bolstered confidence in your ability to adapt to those changes. My system of investing with an economic LEAPS strategy is more suited to these uncertain times than any other model I have come across. Rooted in common sense, it will help you to succeed on the New Wall Street.

Stay in touch with me through the Internet. I try to answer all e-mail through my Web sites, and I'm keenly interested in your feedback. Don't be a stranger! Let's be alpha interactive. Happy hunting.

NOTES

Introduction

1. Leander Kahney, *Inside Steve's Brain*, Portfolio/Penguin Group, New York, 2008, pp. 192–195.

2. TED: Ideas Worth Spreading, "J.J. Abrams' Mystery Box," TED Talks www.ted.com/talks/j_j_abrams_mystery_box.html, March 2007.

3. Atika Shubert and Doug Ganley, "Real David Frost Remembers Fascinating Nixon," www.cnn.com/2009/SHOWBIZ/Movies/01/05/david.frost/, January 5, 2009.

4. Mark Sunshine, "Mark-to-Market Accounting: The Boogeyman of the 1930s Is Back," www.stockwire.com/articles-mainmenu-238/1419-mark-to-market-accounting-the-boogeyman-of-the-1930s-is-back.

5. Steve Jamison, *Wooden*, Contemporary Books, Chicago, 1997, pp. vii–x.

6. Ibid., pp. xi–xii.

7. Joseph Ellis, *His Excellency George Washington*, Knopf, New York, 2004, p. 111.

8. David McCullough, *1776*, Simon & Schuster, New York, 2005, p. 289.

9. Vin Scully, "Baseball America Quotes," en.wikiquote.org/wiki/Vin_Scully.

10. Dan Brown, "Bio," http://www.danbrown.com/#/author/bio.

Chapter 1

1. Jason Schwarz, "Forget $100 a Barrel—Oil Will Plummet to $30," seekingalpha.com/article/91100-forget-100-a-barrel-oil-will-plummet-to-30, August 15, 2008.

2. CBS News, *60 Minutes Special Report*, "Speculation Affected Oil Price Swings More Than Supply and Demand," www.cbsnews.com/stories/2009/01/08/60minutes/main4707770.shtml?tag=contentMain;content Body, January 11, 2009.

3. Jason Schwarz, "Bank of America Is Going Back to $20," www.thestreet.com/p/_search/rmoney/banking/10465278.html, February 20, 2009.

4. James Altucher, "Goldman Doom and Gloom," www.thestreet.com/p/_search/dps/cc/20090325/columnist conversation1.html#entryId10477246, March 25, 2009.

5. Day Trading Stock Blog, "Meredith Whitney, CNBC, 3/10/09," daytradingstockblog.blogspot.com/2009/03/meredith-whitney-cnbc-31009-march-10.html, March 10, 2009.

6. Rev.Shark, www.thestreet.com/p/_search/dps/cc/20090302/columnistconversation1.html#entryId10467129.

7. Alan Greenspan, *The Age of Turbulence*, New York, Penguin Press, 2007, back cover.

8. Michael Inbar, "Jim Cramer: Time to Get out of the Stock Market," NBC *Today*, www.msnbc.msn.com/id/27045699/, October 6, 2008.

9. Maggie Mahar, "'Buy-and-Hold' vs. 'Market Timing'" Bloomberg News, *Journal Record*, Oklahoma City, findarticles.com/p/articles/mi_qn4182/is_19980915/ai_n10121409/, September 15, 1998.

10. James Cramer, *Jim Cramer's Real Money: Sane Investing in an Insane World*, Simon & Schuster, New York, London, Toronto, Sydney, 2005, pp. 15–16.

11. J. Michael Advisors, "Buy & Hold: Myth or Truth?" jmichaeladvisors.com/articles/myth-of-buy-and-hold.htm, Dallas, Texas, 2009.

12. Warren Buffett, "Warren Buffett's Partnership Letter for 1961," www.gurufocus.com/news.php?id=7670, January 24, 1961.

Chapter 2

1. Mike McNamee, "The SEC Has Words of Warning for Online Investors," *BusinessWeek*, www.businessweek.com, January 27, 1999.

2. *E*TRADE FINANCIAL Corporation Fourth Quarter 2008 Results*, investor.etrade.com/releasedetail.cfm?ReleaseID=380284, January 2009.

3. *TD AMERITRADE Corporation Fourth Quarter 2007 Results,* www.amtd.com/investors/webcasts.cfm, January 2008.

4. E. Feldman, "Risk Management Watch: Hedge Funds Focus on Risk as Assets Grow," blog.aefeldman.com/2008/07/01/risk-management-watch-hedge-funds-focus-on-risk-as-assets-grow/, 2009.

5. Isabelle Clary, "Study: Hedge Funds Fuel Market Volatility," www.investmentnews.com/apps/pbcs.dll/article?AID=/20080505/REG/590553837&template=printart, May 5, 2008.

6. Jason Schwarz, "The Bubble of Uncertainty Is About to Burst," seekingalpha.com/article/124520-the-bubble-of-uncertainty-is-about-to-burst, March 6, 2009.

7. Jeremy Atack and Peter Passell, *A New Economic View of History,* 2d ed., New York, Norton, 1994, p. 648.

8. Edward Lampert, "Sears Chairman Edward Lampert's Letter to Shareholders," archives.chicagotribune.com/2009/feb/26/business/chi-biz-sears-edward-lampert-letter-feb26, February 26, 2009.

9. Reuters, New York, "Standard & Poor's Reports January Index Returns." www.reuters.com/article/pressRelease/idUS235870+01-Feb-2008+PRN20080201, February 1, 2009.

10. Yahoo! Finance, "S&P 500 Index Historical Returns," finance.yahoo.com/q/hp?s=%5EGSPC.

11. Jokes News, "Elevator Anxiety," www.jokes-news.com/2006/11/16/elevator-anxiety/.

Chapter 3

1. *Investopedia Dictionary*, "Gross Domestic Product (GDP)," www.investopedia.com/terms/g/gdp.asp.

2. Investment Company Institute, "Research and Statistics," www.ici.org/research; and AMG Data Services, AMG Database of Fund Flows & Holdings, www.amgdata. com/#create:home:Home:/php/signup_trial.php.

3. U.S. Department of Labor, "Labor Force Statistics from the Current Population Survey," www.bls.gov/cps/.

4. U.S. Department of Labor, "Overview of BLS Statistics on Inflation and Prices," www.bls.gov/bls/inflation.htm.

5. Conference Board, www.conference-board.org/; and University of Michigan and Reuters, Surveys of Consumers, Ann Arbor, Michigan, www.sca.isr.umich.edu/.

6. Associated Press, "Bush: Our Entire Economy Is in Danger," www.msnbc.msn.com/id/26871338/, September 25, 2008.

7. Maria Bartiromo, "Talking Ourselves into a Recession," CNBC, Truveo, in.truveo.com/Talking-ourselves-into-recession/id/1874316412, February 10, 2008.

8. Peter Lee, "China Discovers Value in the IMF," *Asia Times*, www.atimes.com/atimes/China_Business/ KF10Cb01.html, June 10, 2009.

9. Conference Board, "The Conference Board Leading Economic Index (LEI)," www.conference-board.org/ economics/bci/pressRelease_output.cfm?cid=1.

10. U.S. Census Bureau News, "Advance Monthly Sales for Retail," www.census.gov/marts/www/retail.html and www.economicindicators.gov/.

11. Titanic-Nautical Society & Resource Center, "Titanic Facts: Everything You Ever Wanted to Know about the RMS *Titanic*," www.titanic-nautical.com/titanic-facts.php.

12. Michael Korda, *Ike*, HaperCollins, New York, 2007, pp. 476–481.

Chapter 4

1. TeachersFirst.com, "Working with Gifted and Talented Students," www.teachersfirst.com/gifted.cfm.

2. *BBC News*, "Buffett Warns on Investment 'Time Bomb,'" news.bbc.co.uk/2/hi/business/2817995.stm, March 4, 2003.

3. CBOE, CBSX, and CFE Press Releases, "Most Active May Ever," www.cboe.com/AboutCBOE/Show-Document.aspx?DIR=ACNews&FILE=cboe_20090601.doc, June 1, 2009.

4. CBOE, "Equity LEAPS Specifications," www.cboe.com/Products/EquityOptions.aspx.

5. David Goodboy, "Using LEAPS to Overcome Options Limitations," TradingMarkets.com, www.tradingmarkets.com/.site/options/how_to/articles/-77279.cfm.

6. Options Industry Council, "Availability of LEAPS," www.optionseducation.org/basics/leaps/leaps_3.jsp.

7. OptionTradingTips.com, "Calculating Historical Volatility," www.optiontradingtips.com/options101/volatility.html.

8. Jennifer Dauble, "CNBC's Becky Quick Sits Down with Bank of America CEO Ken Lewis," *CNBC's Squawk Box*, www.cnbc.com/id/30011937, April 2, 2009.

9. E*TRADE Q1 2009 Earnings Call, http://seekingalpha.com/article/133780-e-trade-financial-q1-2009-earnings-call-transcript.

10. David Lieberman, "IMAX Makes a Dramatic Comeback," www.usatoday.com/money/media/2008-05-05-imax_N.htm, May 9, 2008.

11. Cover story, online extra, "James Cameron on the Cutting Edge," *BusinessWeek*, www.businessweek.com/magazine/content/07_14/b4028005.htm?chan=search, April 2, 2007.

Chapter 5

1. Alice Schroeder, *The Snowball*, Bantam Books, New York, 2008, p. 1.

2. Allstair Barr, "Hedge Funds Try to Hold Back Redemption Wave," www.marketwatch.com/story/hedge-funds-try-to-hold-back-wave-of-investor-redemptions, November 28, 2008.

3. Shamim Adam, "Global Financial Assets Lost $50 Trillion Last Year, ADB Says," Bloomberg, www.bloomberg.com/apps/news?pid=20601087&sid=aZ1kcJ7y3LDM, March 9, 2009.

4. Mark Hulbert, "Can You Beat the Market? It's a $100 Billion Question," *New York Times*, www.nytimes. com/2008/03/09/business/09stra.html, March 9, 2008.

5. Joshua Brockman, "Q&A: Madoff Case Puts Spotlight on SEC," National Public Radio, December 17, 2008.

6. 1986 Nobel Peace Prize Press Release.

7. Portfolio Staff, "Wiesel Lost 'Everything' to Madoff," www. portfolio.com/executives/2009/02/26/Elie-Wiesel-and-Bernard-Madoff, February 26, 2009.

8. Greg Linden, "Yahoo CEO Carol Bartz on Personalization," Geeking with Greg, glinden.blogspot.com/2009/06/yahoo-ceo-carol-bartz-on.html, June 1, 2009.

9. Kevin Kelly, "The New Socialism," *Wired* magazine, Howard S. Mittman, Condé Nast Publications, June 2009, pp. 118–121.

Chapter 6

1. Robert Longley, "Mr. Gorbachev, Tear Down This Wall!" About.com, usgovinfo.about.com/od/historicdocuments/a/teardownwall.htm.

2. Douglas Brinckley, *The Reagan Diaries*, HarperCollins, New York, 2007, pp. 4–5.

3. Ibid., p. 7.

4. Janice Connell, *The Spiritual Journey of George Washington*, Hatherleigh Press, London, 2007, pp. 19–20.

5. Daniel Schacter, *The Seven Sins of Memory*, Houghton Mifflin, Boston, 2001, pp. 12, 112, 138.

6. Mark Sellers, "So You Want to Be the Next Warren Buffett? How's Your Writing?" www.beearly.com/pdfFiles/Sellers24102004.pdf, 2007.

7. Dan Gilgoff, "New Survey: Those with No Religion Fastest Growing Tradition," God & Country, www.usnews.com/blogs/god-and-country/2009/03/09/new-survey-those-with-no-religion-fastest-growing-tradition.html, March 9, 2009.

8. Wikipedia, "Pinocchio," en.wikipedia.org/wiki/Pinocchio.

Chapter 7

1. Council of the Arts at MIT, Synesthesia Introduction,. web.mit.edu/synesthesia/www/ October 7, 1997.

2. Mark Sellers, "So You Want to Be the Next Warren Buffett? How's Your Writing?" www.beerly.com/pdfFiles/Sellers24102004.pdf, 2007.

3. SustainableBusiness.com, News, "Pickens' Mesa Power Places Massive Orders for GE Turbines," http://www.sustainablebusiness.com/index.cfm/go/news.display/id/16023, May 15, 2008.

4. David Cho, "A Few Speculators Dominate Vast Market for Oil Trading," www.washingtonpost.com/wp-dyn/content/article/2008/08/20/AR2008082003898.html?hpid=topnews, August 21, 2008.

5. Josh Loposer, "GM: 1,000 Hydrogen Cars in California by 2014," www.greendaily.com/2008/04/03/gm-1-000-hydrogen-cars-in-california-by-2014/, April 3, 2008.

6. Stanford Report, "New Global Wind Map May Lead to Cheaper Power Supply," news-service.stanford.edu/news/2005/may25/wind-052505.html, May 20, 2005.

7. Jason Schwarz, "The Peak Oil Myth: New Oil Is Plentiful," seekingalpha.com/article/82236-the-peak-oil-myth-new-oil-is-plentiful, June 22, 2008.

8. Bespoke Investment Group, "Revisiting the Home-builders," bespokeinvest.typepad.com/bespoke/2007/10/revisiting-the-.html, October 29, 2007.

9. Bespoke Investment Group, "Bubbles: The More They Go Up, the More They Go Down," bespokeinvest.typepad.com/bespoke/2008/12/oil-the-more-they-go-up-the-harder-they-fall.html, December 19, 2008.

10. Charles Mackay, *Memoirs of Extraordinary Popular Delusions and the Madness of Crowds*, Richard Bentley, London, 1841, chap. 3.

Chapter 8

1. CNN, "The Aftermath of Katrina," September 3, 2005.

2. Yahoo Finance, Dow Historical Results; finance.yahoo.com/q/hp?s=%5EDJI&a=08&b=1&c=2001&d=00&e=15&f=2002&g=d&z=66&y=66

3. Eric Dash, "$75 Billion Fund Is Seen as Stopgap," *New York Times*, www.nytimes.com/2007/11/01/business/01siv. html?pagewanted=print, November 1, 2007.

4. Jeanne Cummings, "Obama Blames Ethic of Greed for Economy," www.politico.com/news/stories/0308/9238. html, March 27, 2008.

5. Testimony of William M. Isaac before the Subcommittee on Capital Markets, Insurance, and Government Sponsored Enterprises, www.house.gov/apps/list/hearing/ financialsvcs_dem/isaac031209.pdf, March 12, 2009.

6. CNBC TV-18 Matrix, Dow Jones History, www.moneycontrol.com/mccode/indices/history.php?indice_ ID=DOWJONES.

7. Amit R. Paley and David S. Hilzenrath, "SEC Chief Defends His Restraint," *Washington Post*, www. washingtonpost.com/wp-dyn/content/article/2008/12/23/ AR2008122302765.html, December 24, 2008.

8. Speech by SEC Chairman: Opening Remarks at SEC Roundtable on Mark-to-Market, October 29, 2008, www. sec.gov/news/speech/2008/spch102908cc.htm.

9. Jason Schwarz, "Time to Exempt Mortgage Securities from Mark-to–Market," www.house.gov/apps/list/hearing/ financialsvcs_dem/isaac031209.pdf, July 15, 2008.

10. AccountingWeb, FASB Responds to Negative Feedback to Proposed FAS 157-e, April 6, 2009, www.accountingweb. com/item/107355.

11. Ian Katz, "Goldman Shareholders Suffered as Blankfein Earned $43 Billion" May 28, 2009. www.bloomberg.com/apps/news?pid=20601109&sid=aOqGBzGEkJbg&refer=home.

12. Barack Obama, "A New Foundation" April 14, 2009. www.america.gov/st/texttrans-english/2009/April/20090414142247eaifas0.3019068.html.

13. Robin Greenwood, "Float Manipulation and Stock Prices," Harvard Business School, July 5, 2006 hbswk.hbs.edu/item/5426.html.

Chapter 9

1. Greg Linden, "Marisa Mayer at Web 2.0," glinden.blogspot.com/2006/11/marissa-mayer-at-web-20.html, November 9, 2006.

2. Margaret Cheny and Robert Uth, *Tesla: Master of Lightning*, Barnes & Noble, New York, 1999, p. 29.

3. Jeremy Atack and Peter Passell, *A New Economic View of American History*, Norton, New York, 1994, pp. 143–145.

4. Nicholas Thompson, "And Data for All," *Wired* magazine, July 2009.

5. Mark McClusky, "Call It Living by Numbers," *Wired* magazine, July 2009.

6. Marshall Kirkpatrick, "The Day Facebook Changed Forever," www.readwriteweb.com/archives/the_day_

facebook_changed_messages_to_become_pulic.php, June 24, 2009.

7. Fred Vogelstein, "The Great Wall of Facebook," *Wired* magazine, July 2009.

8. Martha Legace, "Social Media Leads the Future of Technology," hbswk.hbs.edu/item/6079.html, November 10, 2008.

9. Mocom2020 Team, "4.1 Billion Mobile Phone Subscribers Worlwide," www.mocom2020.com/2009/03/41-billion-mobile-phone-subscribers-worldwide/, March 27, 2009.

10. Nick Wingfield, "iPhone Software Sales Take Off: Apple's Jobs," online.wsj.com/article/SB121842341491928977.html, August, 11, 2008.

11. Cheny and Uth, *Tesla*, pp. 49, 98–99.

12. Seth Weintraub, "Live-Blogging the Apple Q4 Earnings Conference Call," blogs.computerworld.com/live_blogging_the_apple_q4_earnings_conference_call, October 21, 2008.

13. "Master the Basics: The Future of the Internet," www.learnthenet.com/english/html/03future.htm.

14. "Next 100: A Dialogue on the Next Century of Energy," www.next100.com/2008/05/.

15. Daniel DeNoon, "First Human Embryonic Stem Cell Study Set," www.medicinenet.com/script/main/art.asp?articlekey=96011, January 23, 2009.

16. John Lauerman, "Google Backs Harvard Scientists 100,000-Genome Quest," Bloomberg, www.bloomberg. com/apps/news?pid=20601082&sid=a9FTNggspOLs, February 29, 2009.

17. Rob Boisseau, "Obama: 3% of GDP for R&D," American Institute of Physics, www.aip.org/fyi/2009/049.html, April 27, 2009.

18. Daniel Lyons, "A Head in the Cloud," *Newsweek*, www. newsweek.com/id/166738, November 1, 2008.

19. Yahoo! Press Release, "Yahoo Partners with Four Top Universities to Advance Cloud Computing Systems and Applications Research," research.yahoo.com/node/2743.

20. Whitehouse.gov, "Remarks by the President at the National Academy of Sciences Annual Meeting," April 27, 2009.

Chapter 10

1. "Another Olympic Secret: Who Was Actually Singing as the National Flag Entered the Stadium?" *China Digital Times*, chinadigitaltimes.net/2008/08/another-olympic-secret-who-was-actually-singing-as-the-national-flag-entered-the-stadium/.

2. Nicholas Cull, "The Range and Impact of Chinese Public Diplomacy Efforts," china.usc.edu/ShowArticle. aspx?articleID=1475, May 20, 2009.

3. "Hu Jintao Calls for Enhancing Soft Power of Chinese Culture," Seventeenth National Congress of the Communist Party of China, english.cpcnews.cn/92243/ 6283153.html, October 15, 2007.

4. *PBS Frontline*, "The Memory of Tiananmen 1989," www. pbs.org/wgbh/pages/frontline/tankman/cron/.

5. United States–China Economic and Security Review Commission (USCC), "China's Propaganda and Influence Operations, Its Intelligence Activities That Target the United States, and the Resulting Impacts on U.S. National Security," www.uscc. gov/hearings/2009hearings/transcripts/09_04_30_trans/09_04_30_trans.pdf, April 30, 2009.

6. Albert Keidel, "Assessing China's Economic Rise: Strengths, Weaknesses and Implications," Foreign Policy Research Institute, www.fpri.org/enotes/200707.keidel. assessingchina.html, July 2007.

7. "China Is a Private Sector Economy," *BusinessWeek*, www.businessweek.com/magazine/content/05_34/ b3948478.htm, August 22, 2005.

8. Libor Krkoska and Yevgenia Korniyenko, "China's Investments in Russia: Where Do They Go and How Important Are They?" *China and Eurasia Forum Quarterly*, vol. 6, no. 1, www.isdp.eu/files/publications/ cefq/08/lk08chinainvestment.pdf, 2008, pp. 39–49.

9. Julian Borger, "David Miliband: China Ready to Join US as World Power," www.guardian.co.uk/politics/2009/ may/17/david-miliband-china-world-power, May 17, 2009.

10. Peter Schiff, *The Little Book of Bull Moves in Bear Markets*, Wiley, New Jersey, 2008, pp. 4–20.

11. "Inside the Dragon," *National Geographic*, May 2008, p. 170.

12. Archive for Sichuan, chinaview.wordpress.com/category/ china/sw-china/sichuan/.

13. Brook Larmer, "Bitter Waters," *National Geographic*, May 2008, pp. 152–169.

14. Hu Xiao, "China to Quadruple GDP by 2020 to $4 Trillion," www.chinadaily.com.cn/english/doc/2004-04/26/content_326242.htm, April 2004.

15. Speech by Chinese President Hu Jintao at Yale University, www.fmprc.gov.cn/eng/zxxx/t259224.htm, April 21, 2006.

16. China.org.cn, "Army to Modernize Its Logistic Sector by 2020," www.china.org.cn/english/China/236931.htm.

17. "China to Launch Space Station in 2020," *China View*, news.xinhuanet.com/english/2008-09/28/content_10129850.htm.

18. Laura Robertson, "China to Have Universal Healthcare by 2020," blogs.cbn.com/chinaconnection/archive/2009/04/06/china-to-have-universal-healthcare-by-2020.aspx, April 6, 2009.

19. "Hu Jintao's Report at the Seventeenth Party Congress," www2.chinadaily.com.cn/china/2007-10/25/content_6204667_3.htm.

20. Jiang Zhuqing, "Hu Calls for Harmonious World at Summit," www.chinadaily.com.cn/english/doc/2005-09/16/content_478349.htm, September 16, 2005.

Conclusion

1. Hugh Nibley, "Enoch the Prophet," mi.byu.edu/publications/transcripts/?id=75.

INDEX

ABOUT THE AUTHOR

Jason Schwarz is the options strategist for Lone Peak Asset Management (LPAM), a registered investment advisory firm located in Westlake Village, CA. Specializing in option LEAPS, he played a key role in helping LPAM's clients manage their way through the 2008 downturn. His articles have appeared on the Web sites Seeking Alpha, Yahoo! Finance, Stock House, and Mac Daily News, and his expertise has earned him multiple appearances on the Fox Business News Network and Business News Network in Canada. Schwarz lives in Highland, Utah.